JOSE I

D0863677

Restaurant

MARKETING STRATEGIES

Dramatically Improve
Your Restaurant Profits While
Spending Less Money

TIMELESS
MOTIVATION
P R E S S

647.795
RIe

TIMELESS MOTIVATION PRESS

ISBN: 978-0-9819351-1-9

Library of Congress Control Number: 2009922818

PRINTED IN THE UNITED STATES OF AMERICA

Table of Contents

LEGAL DISCLAIMER   5

NOTE   7

INTRODUCTION   9

CHAPTER 1: THE RULE OF SINCERE CARING   21

CHAPTER 2: YOUR UNIQUE SELLING PROPOSITION
    (USP)   51

CHAPTER 3: ZERO RISK TRANSACTIONS   77

CHAPTER 4: WHY YOU MUST HAVE A STRATEGIC
    MINDSET   103
    YOU NEED TO HAVE A VISION IF YOU WANT TO SUCCEED   103
        Vision   105
        Strategy   109
        Operations   116
        Strengths   120
        Your Priorities   126
        What kind of clients do you want?   127
        Vision   133
        Strategy   135

CHAPTER 5: LEVERAGE   137
        Operations and Employees Leverage   138
        Sales and Marketing Leverage   142
        Test Your Marketing   143
        Other Leveraging Possibilities   150

CHAPTER 6: BARTERING   163
        One to One Bartering   166
        Triangulation Bartering   170
        Other Bartering Possibilities   184

CHAPTER 7: GEOMETRIC GROWTH   **191**
    The Only 3 Ways to Grow Your Business   192
    Exponential vs. Linear Growth and Why You Want to
       Grow Exponentially   196
    Areas of Improvement   197

CHAPTER 8: INCREASING THE NUMBER OF CLIENTS   **217**
    Lifetime Value of a Client   220
    Attracting New Clients   224
    Coupons   226
    Targeted Mailing   230
    Join Ventures with Other Businesses   236
    How to Setup a Formalized Referral System   238

CHAPTER 9: INCREASING PURCHASE AMOUNT   **253**
    1.- Increase the Price of Your Menu Items   254
    2.- Increase the Number of Menu Items That You Sell.   255
    3.- Sell Additional Merchandise   259
    4.- Start/Promote a Catering Business   268

CHAPTER 10: INCREASING FREQUENCY OF VISITS   **273**
    3 reasons why a client may stop going to your restaurant   274
    How to Bring Back Your Clients: 275
    What do we do with our client's information?   285

AFTERWORD   **327**

INDEX   **335**

Legal Disclaimer

Thanks for reading all this legalese!

Note:

All the hyperlinks contained in this book are valid and working at the time of publication.

However, as you already know, the Internet is a moving target and some web sites may have changed or updated their links by the time you read this book.

In order to keep the links useful, I've created a page in my website where I will keep all the links updated and working. It will also facilitate for you to access these resources by just clicking on the links without having to type the URL in your browser.

Please visit: www.myrestaurantmarketing.com/book/links.html for a complete list of all the links mentioned in the book.

If you find that some links are not working or if you find some errors, mistakes or omissions in the book, I would really appreciate if you could email me at jose@riescoconsulting.com with your valuable feedback.

Thank you very much for your help and understanding.

Sincerely,

Jose L Riesco

Introduction

Why do I need yet another Restaurant Marketing Book?

So you've just opened your restaurant.

Congratulations! But you are overwhelmed with all the responsibilities and challenges that come with a new business. Now you only need to fill it with customers and count the money... if only this was easy!

Or perhaps you have had your restaurant running for a few months or years now. You know all you need to know about how to run the kitchen, deal with the distributors, keep your books and your P&L updated, and manage the front of the house all while you keep your customers happy.

Chef, Sous-Chefs, Cooks and Helpers, Host, Runners, Busboys and Waiters all follow your directions and the customers seem happy... but you wonder why the restaurant, YOUR restaurant is not always packed?

How come some days for no apparent reason you see many empty tables?

Why do some restaurants in the area seem to be always filled with people waiting in line or making reservations (some time months in advance), while your place that offers great food at good prices is not that popular?

The answer my friend lies in your marketing (or lack of it).

Marketing is the lifeblood of any business and many business owners, especially restaurant owners, underestimate the impact that marketing can bring to your business (I should know, I used to own a restaurant myself and marketing wasn't in the top of my list of important things to take care of). They either don't do much about it, or they just follow the same old, ineffective and expensive ways to market their business: ads in daily or weekly local papers, offer some coupons and place ads in the Yellow Pages.

Of course, good food, excellent service and fair prices are all key components of the restaurant business, but clients (we'll call them clients and not customers from now on, I will explain later) are finicky consumers.

They have busy lives, they don't know your restaurant, or if they do they soon forget about you, about your business. They are not loyal (at least until you make them, I will tell you how), they eat in many places; just like children, they have short memory spans; they get distracted by other places, brand-new places, fancy places, or just convenient places to eat.

The offer is very large and competition is fierce. You need to have something special that can attract them to *your* place, to *your* restaurant. This is what we call in marketing the USP or Unique Selling Proposition. (I will tell you how you can develop your own customized USP in Chapter 2).

Why should a client go to your place and not to somebody else's? This is one of the key questions that we will work on later when, together, we create YOUR marketing plan.

A restaurant is a business. It is a great business. It is a social business and it makes people happy. It is probably one of the best businesses that you can own; but, in the end, it needs to be run as a business. It needs to be profitable, make both the client and yourself happy, and use the same rules and principles than the big boys use in corporate America and all over the world.

Marketing, Sales and Operations are three cornerstones of your business, and **all** of them need to be effective and run smoothly for your restaurant to be successful.

You are not only the Restaurant owner; you are also the CEO of a company. And you owe to yourself, your staff, and to your clients to run the company the most efficient and profitable way that you can.

You need to strive for excellence and you should apply and follow the same rules than other successful businesses do.

I used to own a restaurant and learned that the hard way. I was never satisfied with my knowledge of the best marketing techniques to make my business better. I didn't like the results that I was getting using the same marketing tools as my competitors. I spent many years reading marketing books and researching techniques that could make a difference.

This is where I can help you. After working for many years in the corporate world (working for one of the most ruthless, most cut-throat and most competitive companies in the world) and having 4 years of practical hands on experience of owning and running an upscale independent restaurant, I've leveraged my unique situation to create the most practical, most useful and most resourceful, down-to-earth, restaurant marketing and promotion machine you can find anywhere.

This book is the result of all those hundreds of hours of studying and taking notes. I've done all the work for you. I've condensed the best and most useful information that I could find for you to use.

This book could be longer but it was designed to be short on purpose. I could add lots of extra information, examples and anecdotes, but I know that you are a busy person and don't have time to read a book full of fluff and good intentions. You will find here the information that you need and nothing else.

In this book, you will discover a treasure of tips, practical recommendations and special strategies that will change your mindset, and will elevate your restaurant to the next level.

You can apply some of its recommendations, you can apply them all - it is all up to you.

I have tried to write material that is meaningful and useful for YOU. Therefore, it is up to you how you use it, but please - I beg you - use it, act on it, and put the lessons that you'll learn in practice.

This material works, I know that it does; but in the end this material, as good as it is, is useless if you don't act on it, if you don't implement it.

Every time that you read it, you will discover something new that just passed you by while reading it before.

I know that reading marketing materials is probably not your cup of tea, but I promise you: if you read this book, your mind will start expanding with new ideas, new tips and techniques that you can easily and inexpensively implement to improve your bottom line, to bring more clients in, to make them happier, and most importantly, to make **you** happier.

I've tried to make the language simple, straightforward and easy to follow. You will find the format easy on the eye, the content attractive and inspiring, and the ideas mind boggling, and some of them, if I may say so, revolutionary.

For example, did you know that there are only three ways to grow your business? It is a very simple, straightforward and logical formula but many restaurant owners are not aware of it. We'll cover this in Chapter 7.

Also, do you know the difference between linear and geometric growth? The implementation of this strategy alone can increase your sales by a factor of 33% minimum! (And I am being conservative, believe it or not).

We will also cover many different marketing strategies like bartering, (direct and triangular), joint ventures, how to deal (or how not to deal) with your competitors, changing your mindset to being strategic (versus being operational as most of the restaurant owners do) and many other critical, yet little known areas to improve your restaurant's results.

The way I have structured this book is in a logical progression. You'll see that the first chapters are very strategic. They constitute the solid foundation needed to implement the improvements and changes that will raise the bottom line of your business. We will cover these improvements later on in the book.

I could start by giving you tips and recommendations, as many other restaurant manuals do, but instead I believe you need to change your mindset first if you want to improve your sales.

For every action there is a reaction. If you don't change the way you think, how you operate, and if you don't change your strategy and your vision, you won't change the results that you get.

"If you continue operating the same way, you will obtain the same results."

This is why it is so important in this book that you read and absorb carefully the first few chapters. Read them several times before you move forward. They are the key to all the changes, to all the improvements that you need to make if you want to grow your sales, your profit and your success.

Each day, read and take notes, re-read and then do the homework (yes, each chapter has homework but don't panic: it is fun and easy to do). Then you will implement in your establishment the knowledge you've got from the last chapter before you move on to the next one.

By the end of the book, you should already be making at least 33% more than you are making now, if you are serious about learning and implement the techniques that I will teach you.

The chapters are not long. They don't need to be. However, they are jam-packed with very useful information that you can apply to your place right away.

I could have added lots of "fluff" as many self-help authors do.

Did you know that you could buy excerpts from most of the Non-Fiction books that boil a 200 to 300 pages book down to 8 to 10 pages of essential content? The rest is just filling, anecdotes, etc. that are not really relevant and make you lose time.

I could have made my book's chapters longer to make them look like they are worthy of a higher price, but I decided that condensing the important information as much as possible, while still retaining the easy-to-read factor, would be the most beneficial to my audience: **I am talking about you - the super-busy Restaurant owner.**

You probably have better things to do than to read about my experiences and my personal anecdotes.

One more thing: each chapter builds on the foundation from the previous chapter so please make sure that you follow the chapters in order, and make sure that you understand and have worked on each chapter before moving to the next one.

This is why you should take your time to understand and absorb the content of the Chapter 1. Once you read it, once you analyze the way that you treat your clients, once you commit to this change, you will be able to easily follow the next chapters until the end.

Since this is a long book packed with useful information, I would suggest you to work on one chapter at the time.

Read each chapter and have handy a notepad or computer to take notes. Customize the ideas to meet your needs. Do your homework and then move on to the next chapter. This is the best way to understand and absorb the material. Use this book as a tool, as **your** tool. Use it as the weapon that will bring your restaurant to the next level of sales and excellence.

Also don't be shy about going back and re-reading any the materials many times.

Repetition is the best way to make sure that nothing falls in the cracks of your memory.

As I said, the information is very condensed and often a single paragraph can mean hundreds or thousands of dollars in new ideas about clients or additional sales.

So, "Is this book for me?" you may be asking yourself.

My sincere answer is: I don't know.

This book is not about giving you a few recommendations so that you can make a quick buck (although it is full of practical ideas that will increase your revenue for sure).

This book is about changing your mindset, about changing the way you think and the way you perceive your business and your clients.

So is it for everybody? No, it is not.

This book is not for everybody and I don't expect everybody to read it, and implement it.

The reason why this book won't work for all restaurant owners is because many people are afraid of change.

Change can be difficult; after all, we are all attached to our routines, to our ways of doing things and changing the way that we operate can be a traumatic experience for some people.

This book will challenge you and the way that you operate in a profound and fundamental way.

Again, think about it: if you operate the same way that you do, you will get the same results that you are getting now.

Only with a fundamental transformation of the way that you do business, of the way that you think and operate, can you make exponential improvements in your sales and your income.

Many restaurateurs won't be able (or willing) to commit to it, to apply the strategies and recommendations contained in this book (however logical, effective and proven they may be).

However, if you are one of the few who do; if you think, after reading chapter 1, that this can work for you, that you get excited and willing to apply what you are learning, and you read and follow all the chapters until the end (even if you only implement one fourth of all the suggestions and recommendations that you will get), I guarantee you that you will elevate your restaurant to a whole new level of excellence.

You will be so far ahead of your competitors that you will leave them wondering what you are doing that they are not - wondering, "What's your secret?"

It is not a matter of spending more money on advertising or even working harder.

It is a matter of changing your mindset, changing your strategy and forever changing the way that you see your clients, your staff, and your providers.

But above all, it is the profound change that you will experience yourself that will make you see your business and your life with a whole new and exciting perspective.

But enough talk. Let's roll up our sleeves and start working on the marketing plan: YOUR marketing plan.

You are about to embark on a unique and very exciting journey that will profoundly change your business life forever.

What do you think? Send me an email with your comments at jose@riescoconsulting.com

Also, don't forget to check the web site: www.myrestaurantmarketing.com, subscribe to the free monthly newsletter and read the blogs, participate in the forums and check other announcements.

Happy sailing…

Jose L. Riesco

Chapter 1:
The Rule of Sincere Caring

Why you truly, sincerely need to love your clients.

Always keep this in mind: Your clients don't go to your restaurant only because you have great ambience or excellent food.

Your clients go to your restaurant looking for an experience. They are looking for a sentiment, a sensation. They want to feel special (we all want to feel special, don't we?) and if you are able to provide them with what they crave the most, this simple fact can totally transform your business.

This is the reason why bad service, or even mediocre service, is such a turn off for your clients. If you provide your clients with excellent food, but they don't get the feeling that you and your staff genuinely care about them, if you somehow don't manage to make this event special, don't manage to make them feel special, then you can be sure that they won't come back to your place. If they do come back, it will be at the most because some friends insisted, or just because your location is convenient. This is not the way to create repeated clients.

Dining in any restaurant - and not only in a fine dining restaurant - is a sensory experience that people usually share with their loved ones. Your clients normally come with their families, their fiancées, dates or friends.

Or they may share a meal with colleagues after a busy day where unfinished business can still be discussed around food and wine.

You may also have single clients, either people traveling for business or who just want to have dinner surrounded by other people so that they don't feel lonely.

In the end and in any way you look at it, eating is a social event that we normally enjoy surrounded by other people.

Get a piece of paper and write down the following sentence (cut it and paste it in a place where you can see it every day, because this is the key for you to understand if you want to excel in your business):

People Buy for Emotional Reasons

Or, in your case, people go to your restaurant looking for an emotional experience.

If clients have to choose between great food and great service, they will always pick the latter. Of course, it is always better to provide with both, but if forced to choose, great service always wins. Your host, your servers, and about everybody in your company who interacts with your clients can make or break their experience.

Think about it. How do you think your clients feel if they go to your place, looking forward to having a great time, just to get it ruined by a rude hostess, a careless waiter or a less-than-exceptional service?

All that anticipation that they brought with them goes down the drain, and they feel frustrated beyond the objective reality of small details that otherwise would have been overlooked if your client was satisfied, because your staff provided poor service or mediocre food and ruined their expectations of a great time.

A frustrated client for sure won't come back, she will probably tell all her friends how bad the place is, and recommend to everybody who crosses her path to avoid it like the plague.

Clients can react very strongly to seemingly unimportant details because they don't rationalize with logic to the facts. Their emotions - their hurt feelings - take over with a response unrelated to the objective truth.

And, by the way, I don't know if you've realized that I am using the word <u>client</u> and not <u>customer</u>. This is for a reason. If you look at the dictionary, customer is defined as "a person who buys goods or services" while client is "one dependent of the patronage or protection of another". Think about it. This is profound.

Any restaurant has customers. They come and go.

Most restaurants spend lots of money trying to attract new customers to squeeze from them all the money they can, for as little effort as possible.

If you want to really succeed, if you want your restaurant to be a place where people want to come back time and again, you need to be different. You need to convert customers into clients who come to your place looking for care, looking for your "protection". Not physical protection but the protection against bad food, against bad service, and especially against a humiliating or uncomfortable experience.

You need to be aware of this. You and your staff need to bend backwards to please these clients who trust you with their money, who trust that you will deliver the emotional experience that they are looking for in your place.

Most restaurant owners fall in love with their place, their own food, their own ambience, they think that they have the coolest place in town... Don't make this mistake; instead, fall in love with your clients. Tell them, or better yet, show them with your food, your service, your excellence that they matter to you, that their well-being is important to you and your staff. Do this and I promise you: you will be rewarded a thousand-fold.

I know that all of this might sound very mystical or metaphysical to you, but trust me it is not. If you please your clients, your clients will come back to your place over and over. They will recommend your restaurant to their families, to their friends, to their business associates.

Nobody wants to recommend or revisit a place where his or her experience was less than excellent. They might come back eventually for other reasons (like for a business lunch or dinner with colleagues. If you provide the least amount of effort towards these people instead of a genuine interest in them, a genuine and sincere experience that makes their dining special or extraordinary, they won't be talking about you and your place. And they won't choose to come back. You will become just one more restaurant where they may or may not go again.

There is also the negative publicity. Statistics show us that one unhappy customer will tell at least 12 friends, relatives and co-workers to avoid a business or service that they tried and they were unhappy or had a bad experience with. And this was back in the "old times" (pre-Internet times), because 12 people were more or less how many they interacted with. These days, however, with the popularity of Web 2.0 and Social Networking, you can multiply the number of people that can get this information by hundreds or even thousands.

There is a famous incident that one customer had with a Dell computer. To make a long story short: this person bought a Dell computer, had problems with it and a less than satisfactory experience with Dell customer support. He is an avid blogger and posted his problems online. Very soon his bad experience invited other people to post negative experiences that they also had with Dell. This blog became very famous and hundreds of thousands of people have read it.

Dell reacted later on and tried to undo the damage, but the company admitted publicly that this incident alone cost them millions of dollars in lost revenue. Perhaps if they took better care of this customer (he never became a client) in the first place, none of this would've happened.

Studies show that people's opinions have 4 times the credibility of any other form of promotion.

The point that I am trying to make here is that happy clients are your best allies and they will recommend your place to anybody. Unhappy clients, on the other hand, can make real damage to your credibility and your restaurant.

It doesn't matter how much you promote your business, how much you blow your own horn and how much money you spend in marketing and advertising, nowadays people will Google your restaurant or read the reviews in www.CitySearch.com ,www.restaurants.com, www.zagat.com or www.Yelp.com before they visit.

If you have negative reviews, even if they are unfair or that particular person just happened to have a bad day, they will have a big impact on many people that won't even give your place a try.

By the way, I encourage you to visit these web sites and read the reviews that people made about your restaurant. You will probably be surprised!

I've extracted some random comments from customers who rated restaurants in Yelp.com. They are very interesting to read because you can see right away what I am talking about here.

Here are some positive ones:

"The owners and all employees are always super-nice. They love working there and they definitely have developed a huge following in the neighborhood."

"This place is wonderful. The service is great and the food is superb."

"Who cares if it's a bit pricey? If you are not going to a street cart for your crepe, and if you are not making them in your own kitchen, then you have assumed responsibility for whatever price your sit-down crepe haven charges for your meal."

"Maybe we were just giddy because it was a perfect spring day. Maybe the Gods were smiling upon us because it was Easter and we tried to be Reflective Humans by attending a Unitarian service. Maybe my main squeeze was just feeling extra playful because I let him buy me a motorcycle jacket and rode over there on the back of his bike. But this was a great experience."

Do you notice any common themes? They all talk about how nice the staff was to them and how well they felt. Even the second quote puts service ahead of the food. In the last one, you can see how her opinion was sensorial; she didn't care about the price because she had a great experience.

Let's now see some bad reviews:

"I must confess, I was greatly disappointed in this place. The service was terrible and the food was off. My wife and I were excited to try this place because it's just around the corner from our house. Honestly, we don't have high expectations, but this place was a flop."

This next one is very interesting:

"If I could, I would give this place 0 stars.

A friend and I decided to try out their prix fixe menu-30 dollars for 3 courses. We got through the seafood salads, and when I received my beef bordelaise, I took a few bites, and then noticed that there was a large piece of paper cooked into my dish. Turns out the paper was a left over from a can label, like a Campbell's soup can label! Well, I guess that makes sense, since the dish was reminiscent of beef stew. After the discovery, my friend and I were done, and a little disappointed that their "showcase" menu item could go so terribly wrong.

We sent our food back, and the server apologetically gave us the bill. To my surprise, the manager wanted to charge us 45 dollars total. I was not about to pay over 20 dollars for a small salad- I took it up with the manager, and he explained rather gruffly that since we ate the salads, we needed to pay for them. But - he was charging us FULL price for small starter salads. I don't care that they had a little seafood in them, they were tiny! When I mentioned that I would blog about the experience, he said he didn't care; that we still had to pay. He walked away, and my friend and I sat there for a minute, stunned. Then he abruptly walked back and muttered that it was OK, he wouldn't charge us.

On our way out the door, he approached us again, and said something like, "This is how a business is run," or other. I explained that had we received a full meal per the prix fixe menu, I would have no problem paying the bill. Then he very adamantly asked us to leave. We were rushed out of there, and I can guarantee you I will NOT return. I have never been treated so horribly. Yikes!"

Well, I think that you see the point. The restaurant owner totally mismanaged the situation in the last quote. In the end, not only did he not get paid, but he was also left with two disgruntled customers who will never go back to his restaurant and who are giving the place a really bad reputation in the forums. And guess what? I know this restaurant and although it is located in a great traffic place, it is almost always empty. It survives just because of its great location that allows it to get new customers all the time (most of which will never go back). And the funny part is that the owner may be wondering why he can't get his place full...

Loving your clients brings you more than avoiding negative publicity or negative word of mouth, much more.

Think about it. When you touch the soul of your clients for just one moment...when you deliver an incredible experience by being honest with them...by showing interest in their lives, their likes and dislikes...by recognizing the special occasion that they come to celebrate, that special person that they are sharing this meal with, that special moment that they are looking forward to remembering...when you do all this, something special will happen.

You will gain their loyalty and their heart forever. They will be your allies, your emissaries. They will promote your business with more credibility that you'll ever be able to buy for a million dollars in any other forms of marketing.

We all are human beings with a genetic predisposition to give back when are given, to respond positively to a sincere and genuine person who cares about us···

As human beings, we are also especially good at detecting insincerity and dishonest sales techniques. Be honest and committed to really caring about your clients, provide them with the highest value that you can give, don't try to fool them with shortcuts, and don't try to take advantage of them.

I remember once when I went with a group of friends to a new restaurant. The food was good and the ambience pleasant. However, because of our number (over twenty people), the owner of the restaurant thought that he could get away with anything, so he kept on opening bottles of wine, we didn't even ask for, and pushing and serving the wine around the (big) table.

Of course we drank the wine, but you know what? We noticed. We noticed that we drank more than we should have and that we paid more that we needed to.

The result is that we never went back to that place again. Now the owner may feel proud of himself - because he pushed the wine and made a killing with us - but in the long run, he lost much more than he won because he had twenty unhappy customers who will never go back to his place and who told many other people to never go there for a party.

So what did he win? He sacrificed a short-term gain for a long-term relationship with us, with his clients who he didn't respect and who therefore won't return the respect, who will never give him the business back.

So think about this principle of excellence, let it sink in your mind until it becomes second nature because this can be the most important commitment, the most challenging, and at the same time the most impactful decision that you can make in your entire business life.

And this is not just a nodding of your head and an approval of a principle. <u>You need to re-engineer your entire business around this profound philosophy if you really truly want to be head and shoulders above your competitors.</u>

This principle relies on one core value that you must have: **integrity**. The whole essence of integrity in your life has to do with how much respect you have for yourself, how much respect you have for your employees, your clients, your food and drink providers, your family and your friends. All these people make up your "inner circle" and contribute to the life you have. If you can show respect to them, they will return that respect. If you don't act with integrity, they will recognize it, and your life will be filled with worries and fears.

How much do you want to live your life <u>without</u> worries and without fears?

True success means being honest and having integrity. Your honesty and your reputation are two key principles that - once lost - take forever to recover.

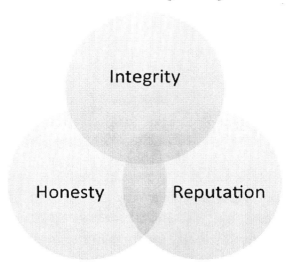

Integrity

Honesty   Reputation

There are three basic components to having a good reputation:

1. **Acknowledge and fulfill any promise that you ever make** or may have made to your clients, your employees or your providers.

2. **Develop an attitude of delivering always more than you promise.**

3. **Always follow up on everything that you do.** This is very important, because people may have different expectations and you may think that you delivered the goods to them while they are expecting something else. That's why it is so important that you always follow up with your clients to make sure that their experience met or surpassed their expectations.

Reputation

Fulfill your Promise	Deliver more than you promise	Follow up

Reputation is just a reflection of how true you are to your word, how sensitive you are to other people's needs, and the value that society gives to your contributions. Your reputation will be judged, **you** will be judged every day of your life.

Multiply whatever one transaction can possible bring you times an infinite number, because that's what you get when you have integrity, when you have a good reputation, when you are true to yourself and sincerely care for others.

Most of the restaurant owners mainly fall in love with their place or with their food or with their concept. The goal is for their restaurant to appear in the Zagat guide so that their ego gets a big boost. They may also worry about their recipes or the appearance of their place.

Let me tell you: they are wrong.

*The way to succeed, to create the greatest
restaurant in the world, is to transfer your passion
away from your place, from your food or even
from your famous chef and instead fall in love
with your client.*

If clients are at the top of your mind all the time, and if all you focus on is constantly getting them the most enjoyable experience that you can provide them with, you will pack your place always with quality clients who will be more than happy to give you their money in exchange for your sincere caring.

It is okay to care about your place, about your food, about having the best restaurant in the world but not with the purpose to feed your ego. The point of your entire place, of your entire business existence is to make your clients happy.

Always ask them for feedback; if you create a great place with great service so that they are happy, they will willingly give you their business and recommend you to all their friends. They will make you happy.

Whenever you have disgruntled clients (and you will since we are all human and make mistakes), make sure to follow up quickly and decisively with them <u>before</u> they leave your place by offering them an appropriate retribution, so that they come back to your restaurant and give it a second try.

It is very important that all your clients and prospects leave your place happy or they will talk bad about you (even if they don't complain in front of you, many people are wary of direct confrontation, but they won't hesitate to talk bad about you to their friends, in forums, at work, etc.

A client who leaves your place unhappy will likely land you a nasty review in <u>www.CitySearch.com</u>, <u>www.Yelp.com</u>, <u>www.zagat.com</u>, <u>www.Restaurants. com</u> or other online restaurant guides.

Make sure to monitor these Web forums on a regular basis (find out which ones are the most popular for your city/region), you will get to know what things people complain about (and often they even mention employees by name, or at least they will describe them, which can help you identify who was their server or hostess).

When you read bad reviews about your place, post a comment in the forums, not only apologizing to the offended clients and offering them appropriate compensation, but – especially - acknowledging that you screwed-up. Period.

Nothing makes people more understanding and willing to forgive than a sincere apology and the acknowledgment of wrongdoing.

If you refute their claims, if you try to confront them or deny what they say (even if you are right), you will only antagonize them more and will lose them forever.

Invite them to come back to your place to give you a second chance, and this time make sure to deliver to them the service and experience that they were looking for and deserve. (It would also be great if you request, after they had a great experience the second time, that they remove their negative comment from the forum).

Try your best to sympathize with your clients and to put yourself in their situation. Don't be condescending and try to mask your unhappiness with the situation. It won't work. Just think that this will happen once in a while (after all, restaurants are people business and people are by nature unpredictable and variable), and that's part of doing business.

The damage control that you can do on the spot to fix the situation - and turn an unhappy customer into a happy client - will pay you a hundredfold by avoiding bad reviews on the web through blogs and restaurant review sites (which can cost you many potential clients); negative opinions to friends, family and coworkers; and perhaps even by converting a disgruntled customer into a repeated client.

Think about a refund as a small investment in the client that can pay itself several times over.

Let's talk now about your other "clients": your employees and your vendors.

First, let me tell you this right off the bat: the more you pay your employees based on their performance (and you can measure performance so that it is clearly superior to the standard) the more you are going to benefit.

Tips are a direct way for clients to reward the server's service, and a good measurement for you.

Excellent service can produce up to a 20% tip and usually increased sales for you. This is a win-win situation. If a server gets consistently tipped lower than the other servers, this is a clear red flag that clients are not really happy with his/her service or that this server is not up to your place's standards.

Talk your staff to find out what went wrong. Sometimes it is the circumstances (one bad day for both parties) but if you see a repeated pattern, then you have a bigger problem. (I will mention later in this Chapter how to address poor performance.)

There are also other factors and other people working for you who don't get the direct benefits and feedback from the tips or online reviews: bus-boys, cooks, runners and other people like janitors, etc. They all directly contribute to the client's experience, and yet are often underpaid and undervalued.

However, as the owner of the place, I bet that you know who performs above and beyond their job description, and who slacks or just barely gets by in their jobs. Don't pay them all the same and don't be afraid to generously reward people if you can quantify their performance.

Smiling and happy employees make smiling and happy clients, and greatly contribute to the well being of the establishment. They make the work environment a pleasant and nice place to be and to come to every day, day after day.

A quick word about your distributors: treat them well, care about them, ask them about their families, their hobbies, their lives. They may seem like just blue collar workers, but they have the power to make your restaurant a priority, to give you the freshest produce, the finest ingredients, or let you know about that extra-fresh fish of the day or a prime cut of meat.

I used to give our providers a sandwich if they were coming mid morning, or some breakfast if they were earlier and I can tell you the difference that this little detail meant to them. I always got some freebies from them and sometimes, when I badly needed something extra, they always went out of their way to deliver it, even at odd times.

And here it goes another gem for you to think about:

The weakest employee that you have sets the standard for your restaurant.

That's right. Read it again: the weakest, lamest employee is the standard for your place. You may have ten excellent people but if you have a single sloppy cook, an uninterested Server, a rude hostess…

That's all it takes for your clients to feel that your place is average or below average.

You should always strive for the highest quality of people that you can get. Hire excellent people, pay them well, treat them with respect and fairness and make them feel as an important part of your company, which they really are!

Happy clients mean big tips and busy business. This translates into more income for you and your employees, as well as a pleasant work environment and ambience for everyone.

I am often surprised about restaurant owners who try to squeeze money from their employees. They may save a few hundred dollars a month in wages and compensation, but they lose the loyalty and happiness of their staff.

These employees (be sure of this) will pass along their unhappiness to the diners and will try to get revenge on the owners.

Don't ever do that! It is not really a good business investment.

For the same reason, if you treat your employees above the market standards, you should expect from them nothing less than excellence.

To help you evaluate your current employees, I've provided you with an "Employee Evaluation Form" at the end of this chapter.

Print a copy and write down the names of all your existing employees on the left column. Then on the right column, assign an evaluation letter from A to D (similar to school grading where A is excellent and F is horrible).

Please don't evaluate your employees based on their current skills but rather based on their aptitude and genuine interest in doing the right thing for your clients and your business. Also, it is very important that you have one-on-one discussions with all of them and find out (if you don't know yet) about their commitment to your place and your clients, about their expectations, their future plans, etc.

Any employee who scores below B should be replaced.

I understand that you may need them for now, but just start planning their replacement as soon as you can and make sure to hire only somebody who can be excellent with your clients. Again, they represent you and your place, and if they are mediocre, your restaurant will also be that way!

So, should you go out of your way to please every single client that steps in your restaurant? The short answer is yes, but with some (minor) exceptions. You should always try to sympathize with your clients, understand their point of view, and provide them with the experience and feelings that they are looking for in your place.

> *However, there are a few occasions (very few) when you have a patron who you don't want to appease like a disruptive client that is making other diner's experiences uncomfortable or unpleasant.*

Let me give you a real example that took place a few years ago, when I still owned an Italian restaurant:

I remember once a customer who came to my restaurant with a date. He wanted to impress his date so he ordered a bottle of Chianti. We opened the bottle, and he tasted it and approved. Minutes later, he called me over and told me that the wine wasn't good. I tried it and it was perfectly OK, but I didn't want for him to feel bad in front of his date. Besides, I could just sell the bottle by the glass so I offered to get different Chianti. We opened a bottle of a different brand. The same thing happened: he tasted it and approved only to tell us that the wine wasn't good a few minutes later.

To make a long story short, we opened 4 bottles of different brands of Chianti trying to please the client. The four were rejected. I approached the man and told him that we couldn't keep on opening bottles and I suggested that perhaps he didn't like Chianti, and we could offer a different variety of wine. He started complaining until a lady seated nearby said aloud that she was a wine expert (she was in the wine distribution business), and offered to sample the last bottle of wine that we opened (according to the disruptive patron was bad). I agreed and let her tried it. She poured it, swirled it around and finally tasted it.

She nodded and said that it was excellent Chianti. The gentleman blushed and got mad. He was mad at me, mad at the lady and basically mad at the world, but - deep down - he was probably mad at himself for trying a wine that he didn't like. He probably wasn't very used to wines, and ordered Chianti because the name sounded familiar. Everybody knows Chianti, right?

The point that I'm trying to make is that this man reacted badly not because the wine was bad or because the service was lousy. It was all in his head. He had this anticipation about how he will order wine and impress his date, about how good the wine will taste, etc. The reality didn't match his expectations, and the whole experience collapsed in his mind. However, he started becoming annoying to us and to the rest of the dinners who were around. He never conceded that he could use help selecting a wine and tried to impose his lack of knowledge on us.

In the end, he didn't leave any tip and left the restaurant upset.

I don't feel like we will miss him. We tried our best to please him and make his experience enjoyable, but nothing was good enough for him, so I guess that we are better off without this kind of customer.

And there you have it.

I encourage you to read this chapter several times and think deeply about it.

If you truly, sincerely believe that the purpose of your business is not to make money but to serve your clients, then you will be ahead of ninety-nine percent of the restaurants around you, and on your way to have an enriching business where your clients, your employees, and your distributors will be happy people.

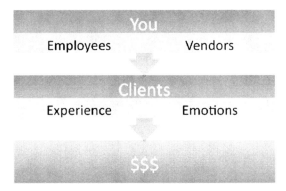

Remember, the clients are the ones who give you the money but before you can get their money, you need to make them happy and willing to give it to you!

In the next chapter, we'll talk about the **Unique Selling Proposition (USP)**. Why you need one and why this USP can differentiate your place from the rest of your competitors, and propel your business to new standards of excellence.

Your clients will love you and your place!

Chapter 3 is even more powerful and ground breaking. It will make your head spin!

But once you are done with it, you will understand how these three first chapters tie nicely together and make a very important and solid foundation for the strategies that we will apply to grow your business exponentially (we will discuss these strategies in detail in chapters 4 through 10).

H O M E W O R K

Employee Evaluation Sheet	
Employee Name	Excellence Ranking (A-D)

Chapter 2:
Your Unique Selling
Proposition (USP)

How you can set your restaurant apart from your competition

So you've got yourself a clean and beautiful place, tastefully decorated, where you serve great food at reasonable prices with good service - as we covered in Chapter 1.

Guess what? There are hundreds of other restaurants nearby that are also nice, also provide good service, and their food is no too bad.

The question that you need to ask yourself is this: "Why should people go to my restaurant and not to these other ones instead?"

In order to stand out among the many other restaurants nearby, your place must offer your clients an advantage over your competitors. If you don't offer something special, something unique, then people don't have any special motivation to go your place instead of other restaurants.

This special offering is called a Unique Selling Proposition (or USP for short), and it is that special something that differentiates your place from every other "me too" restaurant.

If you want to differentiate your restaurant from your competitors, you need to have a USP.

You need to dedicate some time, and think hard about this. You must identify what kind of unique offering your restaurant can provide to your clients.

- What are you the most proud of about your restaurant?

- What is special about your place, your food, and/or your service?

Think about it. After all, when you opened your restaurant you must have done it for a reason.

Didn't you open your restaurant so that you could offer something different - or better – than what was already available? Something special? If so: this could be your USP.

Once you get it, once you know what's special or different about your place from any other restaurant, don't be shy about promoting it. Put it on all your collateral materials; on your website (we'll talk later about your presence in the Web); on your business card, your postcards, your newsletters; tell your staff about it, tell your clients, your providers, your banker; tell your lawyer and your CPA, tell the whole world about that unique factor that differentiates your place from all the other establishments, that factor that makes your place special and different.

But don't just use it for marketing purposes.

You need to adopt and live your USP, or it won't really mean anything.

Developing, identifying and incorporating your restaurant USP into everything you do is challenging but the reward will be worth the time and effort. It will give you differentiation and advantage from any other run-of-the-mill restaurant out there.

CREATING A UNIQUE SELLING PROPOSITION (USP)

To start, your USP must be part of your marketing offering. It must describe one or more of the following items:

- Service

- Quality

- Exclusivity

- Price

- Any other aspect of your restaurant that makes it different from your competitors.

There are many possibilities for coming up with a fresh and original USP. You can position yourself as the restaurant with the largest selection of wines, or the freshest ingredients, or organic dishes, or many different special menus that change every day...

Price is a sensitive one. You don't want to position your restaurant based on the cheapest price (unless you want to compete in the fast food market). It is probably better to offer the finest meals at a higher - but still reasonable - price. However, you can still use price to your advantage: if you offer a lower wine markup than your competitors, for example; or cheaper cocktails as a way to attract potential clients.

You could offer something less expensive (even at your cost) so that people come to your place and then order more expensive items.

Another possibility for a USP is to focus on your clientele. If you want to attract businesspeople for example, you could position your restaurant as the "Best place to host a business lunch or dinner" and elaborate by stating that yours is not a family restaurant where noisy kids can disturb important conversations, and that you understand that business people need time to talk over food and they don't like to get hurried out of the place to make space for somebody else (by getting the bill together with the main dish, as it happens in some restaurants).

Of course, the opposite can also be true. You may decide that people in your area rush to have a quick lunch and go back to work in their offices, so your

USP could be "great and fast quality food" where you guarantee that they can eat in your place in a half an hour or less, but still enjoy great tasting and healthy food.

As you can see, the possibilities for creating a USP are endless. It is best, however, to adopt a USP that addresses a gap that you can identify in your main competitors, and that you can fill. Please keep in mind that, once you commit to a USP, you can get more damage than good done if you are not able to fulfill your promises. Your clients will be very disgruntled if they go to your place because of your advertised USP just to find out that you don't live up to your promises.

Think how much damage to your reputation and your business unhappy clients can cause you.

I can guarantee that if you go around, and ask the owners of the restaurants in your area to describe in one sentence their USP, most will look at you with empty stares. They never thought about what makes their place special. They have the mentality: "I will open a restaurant and hungry people will come", or at best: "my food is good and my prices right, so these should be enough reasons for people to come".

So these people, these restaurateurs don't promise anything with a different value, benefit or service.

They just tell their customers, come here and eat in my place, for no special reason.

It is not a surprise that most restaurants merely get by, struggling to fill their places, spending incredible amounts of money in advertising that doesn't work, to attract customers that they can't keep. Or, if they are lucky and they are located in a convenient place, they get food traffic.

Hungry people will go once to any place but they may or may not go back, depending on how well their needs were met, and how good their experience was at that restaurant.

Clients expect special consideration and treatment in exchange for their loyalty and their money.

Most of the restaurant owners are very good at operations and tactical management; they know how to run the daily routines to keep the business rolling. However they are really bad at strategy and positioning. This is where you can get an edge, a big advantage that will put you head-and-shoulders over your competitors.

Compared to all these things that I've mentioned so far: real, deep and sincere caring about your clients, your staff and your providers, creating and living a Unique Selling Proposition (USP) may look like a pie in the sky theory to many restaurateurs (who are usually down-to-earth, tactical people worried about the day to day operations), but I can assure you that if you manage to make them as fundamental cornerstones of your business, they will make your restaurant unique and position your business way ahead of your competitors.

So, now that you are convinced about the advantages of having a USP (because you are, aren't you?), let's go to the next step and see how you can create your Unique Selling Proposition.

To develop your USP you will need to go through several steps. These steps include gathering information, adding some writing and seasoning with a pinch of creativity.

I will give you first the steps so that you will understand the concept, and then you can use the homework template, located at the end of the Chapter to help you create your own USP. In the homework,

I've added some examples of USP that you can use as a source of inspiration for your own business.

USP Step by Step

These are the steps:

1. **Ask yourself what in your establishment is different (or how your business is different from those of your competitors)**: What is it that truly makes your place different, and is the reason your clients go to your restaurant instead of your competitors.

   When determining your USP take the following points into consideration:

   - **Value and quality of your offerings.** You must be original. Do you offer a "satisfaction guaranteed or your money back" promise? This could be a point of difference, **the main point of difference**, so you should seriously consider it (we will talk in length about this idea in the next chapter).

   - **Your ambiance:** Is it the décor, fixtures and art, or perhaps it may be the menu or a unique menu item that could become the USP? For example, do you have a signature dish that people come to your place for? Perhaps the best Italian wine selection in the area, etc?

- **Location of the business:** You know the famous real estate phrase: Location, location, and location. Write down a number of unique points about the location of your business if it's any good, but don't limit yourself.

  Perhaps your location is not beautiful and you don't have a great view, but it **may be convenient** because you have lots of offices or businesses around. Or perhaps you have a big parking lot and your clients can park without a problem, while in other restaurants they have to struggle to find a spot or even have to pay for parking. Use it to your benefit: describe it as a convenience for your clients, and a part of your USP.

2. **Ask your clients:** You may know most of your clients anyway, so it should be easy. All you need to do is sit down with them for five minutes and ask them the question "Why do you come to my restaurant?" You will soon find out some relevant information of what your

USP could be. Ask between 10 – 20 customers to get a broad range of ideas.

3. **Ask your staff:** Ask them the same questions you asked yourself and your clients: what's good about us? What's special about us? Ask them to comment about your place: the décor, the food, the service, your beverages and location.

4. **Ask your providers:** They are exposed to many restaurants since they deliver food to them. They can see objectively what's special about your place, and if you follow the rule of sincere caring with them, they will be happy to help you and tell you what's unique about your place.

So basically you need to identify what needs are being unfulfilled by the restaurants that directly compete with yours (because of proximity or similar kind of food, etc.). In the Homework section at the end of this chapter, I've included some points that can help you find your USP.

The main point is to focus on one niche or gap that your competitors don't offer. And remember, you must keep any promises that you make!

http://www.myrestaurantmarketing.com

5. **Once you have all this information in front of you, try to find some common themes and statements from you, your clients and your team.**

Your USP will differentiate you from your competitors. It will be the baseline of all your marketing, letterheads, Web presence and business cards. It will drive all your future marketing and communications for your restaurant. Your USP will - at a quick glance - tell your clients and prospects who you are and what's special about your place.

Also keep in mind that your USP won't appeal to all clients and that's OK. You need to decide when you create your USP, the market segment that you want to focus on.

Do you have a really big place, and do you want to attract many customers because volume is important to you? Then your USP should focus on low prices, fast service (so that you can move people quickly, etc.). Of course, this approach won't attract upscale clients - but that's OK, you can't be everything to everyone.

On the other hand, you may want to focus on a small but selective group of people and target your USP specifically to the likes or interests of this audience. Then low prices won't be a compelling USP; your focus should be instead on service, on ambience, on exclusivity...

So you thought hard and long, and finally have a good idea for a USP. Now what?

6. You need to articulate your USP crisply and clearly to have an impact.

It can't be too long (or the message will get diluted) or too short (it needs to explain clearly what you offer). Don't try to be too creative or too abstract.

You should be able to articulate your USP in one paragraph or less.

Think about the USP as the core around which your whole business will be built, so you'd better choose it carefully.

What could you have as a USP, so that when somebody wants to go to a restaurant your place is the first one that comes to his or her mind?

Think about your own personal experiences: If you are in the market for a product or service, wouldn't you prefer to go to a business that has a clear and compelling USP instead of a "me too" approach?

The creation of a USP is a very good step, but not the end of the race.

7. You need to communicate your USP to your employees.

If you and your people don't have a crystal-clear recognition or understanding of your USP, your clients won't have it either.

It is very important that all your staff, from waiters to runners to hosts to bussers to your kitchen personnel, is aware of and sincerely believes in your USP. They are the ones who interact with your clients, your providers, and your service people. They are the emissaries of your business.

If they don't believe your USP, if they are not convinced that you really mean it; if they think that it is something that you say but don't practice, your message can backfire.

Instead of having your staff as your allies and representatives of your business, they can become your harshest critics, and they will make sure than many other people know about you and your company's weakness.

So once you've created a really good USP, and all your employees and providers know about it and believe in it, there is still one last step that you must take:

8. **Build your USP into all your promotional and marketing materials (including advertisements, newsletters, website, postcards, coupons, etc.) to express its basic premise.**

   This is a very important step. After all, the point of having a USP is to make sure that people know about it. Your USP will differentiate you from your competitors, and will make your place attractive to current and future clients, so you need to spread the word; you need to use your USP in all your communications and marketing materials.

   Also, you can use the USP together with special coupons or promotions, so that your customers get a reminder of your Unique Selling Proposition - and your restaurant is engraved in their minds.

   And remember that your promotion or offering has to be consistent with your USP. So if you have a USP targeted to upscale clients, don't just mention in your special offer a cheaper price. This is not what these specific clients are looking for, or at least this is NOT THE ONLY THING that they are looking for.

Instead, just mention that if it is their anniversary or birthday, or you are hosting an extraordinary wine tasting event, (or any other occasion or reason to bring them back to your place), you thought that they would enjoy a discount in your special menu, or that you will reserve the best table in the restaurant for them, or something that will make the event special and memorable.

Also, don't forget to mention that this promotion, or offer, is available ONLY to selected clients (or even only to that person, if you are targeting a special occasion like a birthday or anniversary, etc.). This will make them feel special, and everybody likes to feel special.

You need to let the world know about your place, and the USP is the best way to do this.

So these are the steps to create a sincere and compelling USP. However, I want to emphasize yet again that having a USP is not marketing gimmick, and you really need to believe in your USP.

THE 2 BASIC RULES FOR YOUR UNIQUE SELLING PROPOSITION

I will give you now two basic rules that you must always remember:

Rule number one

1. *ALWAYS SELECT A USP YOU KNOW YOU CAN DELIVER UPON.*

Your clients will hold you to your promises, even if they don't say a word if you don't deliver on your USP. People expect promises to be kept, they want results; they don't have any interest in your problems or excuses.

Many of your clients won't complain directly to you, even if they feel cheated and leave your place disappointed because they were expecting what you promised in your USP and they didn't get it. They will simply stop going to your place and start looking for another restaurant where they feel that they can get what they expect, even if it is less than it was promised by your place.

Rule number two

2. *YOU AND YOUR EMPLOYEES MUST LIVE, EXPERIENCE AND ACT UPON YOUR USP AT ALL TIMES.*

So talk often about your USP, train your new employees, ask them to explain it to you, so that you know if they get it and, especially, live your USP. You are the role model for your staff and they will look at you to see if you walk the walk or just talk about it.

Unique Selling Propositions are not a new idea. Many industries use them effectively in their marketing. For example, these are three of the most memorable USP's from very well known companies:

M&M's were one of the first sugarcoated chocolate candies on the market. They created a great USP:

- *"It melts in your mouth, not in your hands."*

There were some other sugarcoated chocolate candies on the market, but the USP made M&Ms stand out from their competitors.

Domino's Pizza grew also because of their unique USP:

- *"Hot, fresh pizza delivered in 30 minutes or less - guaranteed".*

As you can see, they weren't afraid to backup their USP with a money-back guarantee if they didn't deliver their pizzas in 30 minutes or less. Did they give away some free pizzas? Probably more than a few, but this guarantee made them the number one pizza company in the world! Since people in a hurry knew that they should get their pizza delivered quickly.

FedEx became popular also because of their USP:

- *"When it absolutely, positively has to be there overnight".*

Again, this was a strong proposition for people who needed to ship things quickly. If you needed to ship something that you knew had to be there tomorrow, whom would you call?

Do you see the power of a great USP? I hope so.

Now we need to come up with a USP for your place. We will do this following the steps outlined in the homework.

But before we get down to creating your own USP, think about this one:

"This is our Guarantee:
If you are not 100% satisfied with your dining
experience, your meal will be free."

Ok, so I know what some of you may be thinking now: "What? Are you kidding me? Free meal if they are not happy?"

Remember what we talked about in the first chapter? Your client is your number one priority.

We will talk in detail about this guarantee, its implications and how can make your business explode with clients and sales in the next chapter!

And by the way, you should also integrate your USP into every contact that you have with your unsatisfied clients.

Whenever a client asks you for a refund (following your commitment of total satisfaction), instead of resenting the fact that you have to give them back the money and lose your transaction, use this opportunity to remind them the essence of your USP.

Articulate your deep dedication to your USP, and apologize for any inconvenience, discontent or unhappiness that they may have felt in your place, for whatever reasons they felt dissatisfied.

In the next chapter, we will talk about Zero Risk Transactions in more detail.

You will see how nicely these three first chapters tie together, and how it makes sense to make your clients an offer that they can't refuse.

HOMEWORK

Make a list of the real benefits or advantages that you already offer to your clients.

- Think about what's special about your restaurant. Is it your food? Your wine selection? Your service? Your location? Your decorations? Do you offer live music? Do you have a large menu selection? Open kitchen? Etc.

- Ask your customers, your employees and your providers what makes your restaurant special or different. Perhaps you have a unique recipe that people really appreciate and come to enjoy, or perhaps your chef comes out of the kitchen and greets the clients, or you have bilingual servers who can communicate with foreign travelers in their own language.

  Some points that can help you find your USP are:

  - A large selection of dishes in the menu

  - Unique, ethnic menu or menu items

  - Restaurant especially designed to accommodate families (with a play area or toys or entertainment for children, etc.)

- Reasonable prices

- Quality of the food

- Originality of the dishes

- Impeccable presentation

- Excellent service (good is not good enough: it must be excellent to make an impact!)

- Wide wine selection or special hard-to-find wines

- Wide beer selection or special hard-to-find beers

- Specialty cocktails

- Open kitchen where people can see/talk to your cooks

- Beautifully decorated place

- Live music

- Candles on the tables

- Cloth linens

- Original art on the walls

- Any other distinct advantage that you may have or can provide that your competitors don't provide.

Make a second list of benefits or special things that your competitors offer and you don't.

- For example, do they have a big place while your restaurant is small? Do they offer a full bar and you don't? Do they have a super-chef that you can't afford? Do they have an excellent location and your place is out of the way?

List the ways that you could improve upon your competitor's unique advantages.

- If their place is big and yours small, you can use this to your advantage by stating that you offer "A unique experience in a small place where you'll receive a very personalized treatment".

- Or the opposite - if your place is large, you can say "We have facilities large enough to accommodate your office party or your special occasion".

- Or you could compensate not having a full bar with offering an extensive and excellent selections of wine.

- If you have a great location, say that you are "conveniently located in the middle of the city, within walking distance from..."

- Or if you are out of the way, you can always say "our restaurant offers free parking and it's worth it the trip since you'll surely enjoy an extraordinary dining experience"... You get the idea.

So write down the top 5 advantages and differentiators that make your place unique, then try to combine them into one short sentence or phrase.

This will become your USP.

So once you come up with your USP, write it down, review it and edit it several times.

- Write your new USP in a one-paragraph statement. You may have problems expressing it concisely and clearly. It may take a few paragraphs. It's OK.

- Now you need to edit down all the fluff (trim the fat) and focus on the core of the message until you have a clear and unique USP that people can recognize and immediately identify with your business. It needs to become one memorable sentence.

- Share it with your employees; share it with your clients. Announce it to the world by using it in all your marketing and sales materials...

So, to conclude, with a concrete example: Let's assume that you own a small restaurant, and want to promote as a USP its unique ambience and special treatment to your clients, so that they feel appreciated and special.

Your USP could look something like these:

"Only 100 clients fit in our beautiful, small restaurant. That's a hundred friends who will be treated like royalty."

"We will make you feel special, whether you dine with us alone
or you come with your friends, family or colleagues.
Guaranteed!"

"Our servers have been specially trained to provide you with an unforgettable dining experience"

In the end, if you can't find any characteristics to use as a USP, make your own one by offering

"Free meal if your dining experience doesn't meet your expectations."

I can assure you that nobody else in the industry does this, and your restaurant will become a place where clients will keep on coming and spending their money. We will talk more about this one in the next chapter.

And above all, LIVE YOUR USP. Make it happen! You won't regret it.

Chapter 3:
Zero Risk Transactions

Make them an offer that they can't refuse

One basic rule of marketing is: Lower the barrier for consumers to make the purchase, so that they are not afraid to complete the transaction. Some well-known businesses like Costco or Nordstrom (from the very cheap to the very expensive) embody this technique by allowing their customers to return the items that they purchase any time, no questions asked. This makes people feel better about buying things on impulse knowing that, if they are not happy with the purchased items, they can always return them and get their money back.

Do people return things? Of course they do, but I can guarantee you that the increased sales that these corporations make because of this guarantee are many times bigger than the relative small percentage of returns that they must accept.

So how can we apply this proven technique to your restaurant? What can you do to entice people to come to your establishment?

WHAT CAN YOU OFFER TO YOUR POTENTIAL CLIENTS TO MAKE YOUR PLACE MORE ATTRACTIVE THAN ANY OTHER RESTAURANT

We talked in the previous chapter about having a crystal-clear, defined USP that you live by. It is very important to make your place noticeable in the eyes of the constantly distracted consumers, so what if you make them a proposition that they can't refuse?

What if the barrier of acquisition (or in your case: walking through the door of your restaurant) is so low and so risk-less that most everybody would be comfortable to make a purchase?

It is always a good idea to put ourselves in the shoes of your clients, so we'll try to analyze what's in their minds.

What fears do you think they have before they walk in your door?

Let's make a list of factors that could affect people negatively, making them decide not to go to your restaurant, and instead give their business to somebody else. These are some of the obstacles in our prospects' minds that we need to remove if we want them to become our clients for life:

1. They may not like your type of food.

2. They may like your type of food, but they may not like how you prepare it.

3. Your prices may be too high, and people are afraid that they will spend the money and not enjoy the experience.

4. The place is dirty or ugly.

5. The servers may be very slow, or rude, or difficult to deal with.

6. Your location is not good or it is inconvenient (perhaps you don't have good parking or the restaurant is far from a highly-populated area).

7. The ambience (decorations, lighting, temperature or music) is not very inviting.

8. They've never been to your place, and they already have a favorite restaurant that they frequent.

They may be some other reasons, but I think that we covered the basics here.

Now, consider that one, a few or most of these factors could be in prospects' minds, and make them decide to dine somewhere else.

HOW TO ELIMINATE THE FEARS OF YOUR CUSTOMERS SO THAT THEY FEEL MOTIVATED AND HAPPY TO COME TO YOUR PLACE

First of all, if any of the issues mentioned in points 2, 4, 6 and 7 is real, it needs to be addressed and fixed right away. There is no excuse for bad food, poor service, or an ugly or uninviting place. (The idea of a dirty restaurant - this is the number one client killer, and nothing else that we do can overcome this big problem.)

We already discussed in the previous chapters how to fix the quality of the food and service issue.

You can address point numbers 2 (your Chef and kitchen staff) and 4 (your waiters and hosts) by analyzing your employees, firing the ones that are hopeless (sorry to be so straight-forward here, but they can really ruin your business if you don't take action), and mentoring and training the rest who have potential, so they understand and live your USP and love your clients

So, assuming that your place is clean and that, perhaps, you can work a little on the ambience (by decorating the place with good taste, adding some artwork, candles, linens, curtains, etc.), and that the service and food are excellent (anything else is not acceptable), then how can you overcome obstacles 1, 3, 5 and 8?

I'm afraid that point number 1 is insurmountable if people don't like the flavors of your particular cuisine - sorry! The good news is that you still will hopefully have plenty of people who will love it.

Regarding points 3, 5 and 8, there is good news for you: This is what the Zero-Risk Transaction is all about.

You need to embed in the minds of your clients that they will risk nothing if they come to your place for a meal.

How?

Well, I mentioned already to put this in your USP, but I will repeat it again since this concept is such an uncommon practice in the restaurant business.

Ready? Here we go!

You offer your clients the following USP proposition:

"We guarantee that your dining experience with us will be excellent or you won't have to pay for your meal."

"What?" you are probably thinking. "Are you crazy? You know how many people will take advantage of this to get a free meal?"

Well, "no" and "probably a few" are the answers to the last two questions; but before we look at the consequences, let's put ourselves in the minds of our potential clients.

Your anniversary (or birthday or other important celebration) is coming, and you want to take your spouse to a nice restaurant to celebrate this happy occasion.

There are many choices, many restaurants and many different world cuisines; in fact, the choices are almost endless.

What can you do to please your spouse?

Most people do one of the following three things:

1. They go back to a restaurant where they had dinner before, and had a pleasant experience (perhaps because they went there when they were dating, or they had dinner there together and it was nice…)

2. They ask a friend, relative or colleague about a good restaurant in town, because they want to try something new.

3. They look at reviews (either a guide like Zagat's, or online at www.Restaurants.com or www.Citysearch.com) to see what other people recommend, searching for the highest rated restaurants.

Now, from these three scenarios, there isn't probably much that you can do with number 1 (memories are memories after all), but if our imaginary couple decides to try something new, you will have a great chance to score with numbers two and three.

Your "Guaranteed Excellent Dining Experience" assures the nervous potential clients that there is no risk involved in going to your place. If they go and don't have a great dinner experience, they won't spend a dime.(And notice that I always mention the word experience and not meal; clients look for an experience, a great moment to share, and not just to fill their tummies.)

This is even better than the money back guarantee that places like Costco or Nordstrom have. Your clients won't even have to pay before leaving your establishment!

*Can you implement this policy before your place
is running smooth as silk?
The realistic answer is NO.*

You first need to improve your processes, beautify your place, encourage your chef (so that s/he performs to the top of his/her ability), and - last but not least - train all your staff so that they can offer the best client service that there is.

Now, I want you to do an exercise that will help you tremendously to improve your business, since it will make you think about what areas of your restaurant are the weakest ones and therefore need the biggest improvement.

You can't offer a free meal if all the key fundamentals of your restaurant: trained staff willing to put clients as their number one priority, great quality of food, right prices, good décor, etc. aren't aligned to meet your client's needs.

So are you still with me? Okay, let's continue.

Imagine for a moment that you've just started promoting your new USP and advertising the *Free Meal if you are not 100% satisfied* guarantee.

You open for dinner and you see many new clients walking through your door because of this guarantee.

Now, put yourself in their shoes and think" in this specific situation, what could be wrong with my experience that will make me demand that the owner must honor this free meal guarantee. Write down all the possibilities.

Your checklist might include:

- Quality of the food

- Quality of the service

- Promptness of seating

- Food delivery time

- How pleasant is the ambience

- Cleanliness of the place

- Attitude and happiness of your servers

- Menu and drinks prices

- The restaurant's unique appeal

- Any other factors you can think of

What elements of this list have you already committed to preserve the guarantee?

Which ones are almost there?

Which ones are you totally missing the mark on?

Focus on the ones that are almost there and the ones that you are missing.

What can you do to bring them up to speed? Perhaps your staff needs training? Do you need to change some menu items? Do you need to change some dishes to make them better, more unique, special?

Do you need to setup policies? Do you need to improve processes so that all your employees always know what to do and how to react in any predictable situation?

You need to be realistic and work on these shortcomings if you want to succeed. Even if you are not planning to give your clients the free meal guarantee, this exercise will help you improve your offering and make your clients happier.

However, once you have all these elements in place, I can assure you that you will be able to fulfill your USP of money back guarantee without any fear.

And speaking of fear: Let's go back to your concerns.

Actually, not only this is not a crazy idea, but I also think that if you implement this policy, your restaurant will be so full of happy clients, that you will have to work overtime to keep up with the demand.

So what about those abusive clients that, even after you believe everything went well, still don't want to pay for their meal?

Well, you'll have to give it to them and suck up the losses.

But (and this is important) this won't happen often, and the lost money is much less than you think.

Actually, you'll probably have less than 1% of the people who'll go to your place asking for a free meal. And even when this happens, the loss of real money is much smaller than the loss of clients because of this patron due to negative reviews posted on websites, and badmouthing your place to their friends and relatives.

Plus, the people who ask you to honor your guarantee (actually they shouldn't even ask you, you should be proactive by offering to resolve the issue) will either come back and you'll have a repeat client, or they won't and then you lose a lousy client who you don't want anyway - in both cases it is a win for you.

There are five main scenarios where a potential client would deserve a free meal:

1. The food was really not good, or arrived very late or cold.

2. The service was bad, rude or slow to respond.

3. Something in your place wasn't up to the client's standards (loud music, their dining area was uncomfortable, the bathrooms or tables were dirty, etc.)

4. An accident happened (spilled food or drinks, broken chair or table, etc.)

5. The customer is a jerk and just wants to take advantage of the free meal guarantee.

Now, from these five scenarios, the first four are the real deal. The clients really want to have a good time and a great experience in your place, but circumstances or incidents didn't allow them to receive what they wanted.

If you didn't have your free meal guarantee policy, they would just leave your place unhappy, they will probably talk badly about your restaurant to everybody, and a big percentage of them will smear your business name across the virtual floor in online blogs, forums, etc.

Now, because of your policy - because you follow up and put your money where your mouth is - they get a free meal, they don't even need to get their money back because they never paid in the first place. So they don't feel cheated or abused, and there is no reason for them to complain or to talk badly about you or your place.

Most likely, these people will come again and thus give you the opportunity to recoup your money.

But there is more.

Because few in the restaurant industry have this incredible USP, they will tell all their friends, relatives, etc. what a great place you have and how you took care of them and fixed their issue.

You see where I am going?

You will convert a negative experience with potential devastating consequences, into a positive spin and inexpensive advertising (for just the cost of the meals).

You will avoid negative feedback, and give no reason whatsoever for anybody to talk badly about your place.

Yes, they may post on the blogs comments like: "I didn't like the food, but they gave me my money back".

Don't you think that when people hear about this, they won't be tempted to try your place?

"Yes, but what about those customers in Group five?" you may be wondering. "Won't they take advantage of the guarantee?" (Notice that I called them customers and not clients.)

Well, as I said, you may have some of these, but the good news is that they will only go to your place once.

After they get their free meal, they won't have the nerve to visit your place and ask for their money back again.

But what if they do? If they do (and of course there may not be a reasonable cause for a repeat event, it may happen that they are just unlucky!), you are morally justified to ask them why they keep on coming to your place if they continue to be dissatisfied, and therefore complete your fiduciary obligations to them (this is a fancy way to say that you won't be doing business with them anymore).

These people will be rare, and would've represented paying customers that you want to avoid anyway.

You are still not convinced?

Let's look at some numbers and you'll see what I mean.

Let's say that you get 100 customers per night and four of them (one unhappy table) ask for a free meal. Your average meal is $40 per person and your profit margin 50% per meal.

In a normal restaurant, these customers wouldn't probably ask for a free meal, since people are not used to get this kind of perk from a restaurant. They most likely would have simply left unhappy and tell everybody how bad their experience was.

So, let's first analyze your losses: 4 meals x $40 = $160, but this is really not the actual loss since your cost would be $80 (50% of the gross sales). Your cost is $80 to make four visitors happy, and, by the way, they most likely will come back to your place and enable you to recoup that loss.

Now let's see what would happen if you charge them, and let them walk out unhappy:

There are studies that prove that one disgruntled customer will tell an average of 12 people about their (bad) experience. These were done, of course, before the age of the Internet.

Nowadays, one bad review can be seen by hundreds (even thousands) of potential clients that may decide to take their dining experience elsewhere after reading the bad comments about your place.

But let's be conservative and follow the "old school" numbers: the four unhappy dinners from our example will directly recommend to 48 people not to go to your place. This means a potential loss of 52 people (including the four unhappy customers).

So this is the math:

52 (customers) x $40 (spent per customer) = $2,080 (gross revenue)

This equals to $1,040 net revenue for you (50% of the total gross) plus $312 in lost tips (assuming a 15% average tip for your wait staff).

So you see? The $80 that you lost for compensating for your customer's dissatisfaction doesn't look that bad, does it?

And there is also an additional benefit here. Most likely, these four clients will tell all their friends, relatives and acquaintances about your place, and how their bad experience was (whatever the reason) but that the problem was quickly and decisively taken care of by you (or your staff).

They will also tell others how it is totally worth it to try your restaurant since there is no risk involved.

(Of course, always find out why the clients are not happy in the first place.)

Was the food late or bad? Was the service poor? Was the place in less-than-optimum condition? Was it untidy? Were the tables, the flatware, the silverware or the restrooms clean enough? Did an accident happen?

It is essential that you keep track of why the clients are not happy.

I recommend that you buy a notebook in which you write down the date, the problem details, and the number of people involved. This will help you enormously to look for patterns. If you see that many different clients complain about the same issue, then you have a problem that you need to address as soon as possible.

This will provide additional constructive feedback that will help your place to excel among your peers.

Also, don't wait for clients to request their free meal. Always be alert. Ask your clients how they feel; notice if they are silent or they look unhappy. Be emphatic with them, and if you see that they aren't very pleased, offer them something to compensate for their dissatisfaction: a free dessert, deduct one of the dishes, etc.

The point is to make your clients very, very happy with your food, your service and your atmosphere.

Remember: Eliminating the risk barrier will bring undecided clients that otherwise wouldn't try your place.

Plus, it will give you a competitive edge, since almost nobody else in the food industry dares to stand by their products and services with a "Guaranteed Great Dining Experience".

If you still have any doubts about this policy, look at it this way:

> *If you don't trust your business enough to guarantee that you can provide your clients with a great dining experience, ask yourself: Why should they buy from you?*

Why should they carry all the risk to go to your place and give you their money?

By taking the risk away from your clients, and putting it on your shoulders, you remove the barrier - the hesitation that they may have to go to your place and give you their money.

They know that they will have a great dining experience and not only because you're telling them so (like so many of your competitors do), but because they know that if something unpleasant happens, they are covered by your guarantee and they don't need to pay for their meal.

They can trust you and can trust your establishment.

They will reward you lavishly with their hard-earned dollars, and they will act as your sales force by telling the people they know, how great your restaurant is and how they should go and try it themselves.

Think about this guarantee as an inexpensive way to recruit the best sales force in the world: *your own clients* using the best advertising that there is: *their referrals and word of mouth*!

Your risk is very small; your potential, almost unlimited.

In the next chapter we will talk about why you must have a strategic mindset.

Most of the restaurant owners run their daily operations without having a plan and a vision, and without ever thinking where they want to go and what they want to accomplish.

It's like going to a trip and just driving around, taking care to follow the traffic rules and driving the car without having a destination.

I will show you how you can create your vision. And why you need to focus on your strengths if you want to succeed and be happy.

As usual, I hope that you found this chapter insightful and full of ideas that you can implement right away.

Please read the chapter again several times and do your homework. It will make a big difference in your business.

H O M E W O R K

1. **Write a "Satisfaction Guaranteed or Your Meal is Free" sentence that you can use in your USP.**

   You may use as a guideline some of the following sentences:

   - *"You'll have an excellent dining experience in our restaurant or your meal will be free, GUARANTEED!"*

   - *"If you are not 100% satisfied with your dining experience, the food is on us."*

   - *"If you are not totally happy with your dining experience, you don't pay a dime."*

   - *"If you don't like our food or service, you don't pay for it."*

   (This one could be a little tricky since you can still charge your clients for the drinks or liquors and only discount the food and the tip; after all, it is part of the guarantee).

   - *Etc.*

2. **Try to capture different scenarios where you'll apply the Satisfaction Guaranteed premise:**

- Describe seven scenarios that, even after you put in place all the right things to do and operate, still can go wrong and make your clients unhappy (this is life after all, and we all know that in real life nothing is perfect).

  I will give you a couple of examples. Add your own in the lines below:

  - The food was burned or tasted overdone.

  - The clients waited for ½ hour to be seated, even after making a reservation.

  - A waiter spilled food or drinks on the table.

  - ---

  - ---

- ---

- ---

- ---
  ----

3. **Think about and write down the not-so-obvious scenarios that might occur, where your clients don't ask you to honor your guarantee** (some people feel really embarrassed about asking for a free meal - especially in front of other people) **but you think that they deserve it anyway.**

Remember, you won't wait for them to ask you, offer it to them and you'll be amazed about their positive reaction. They don't expect this level of attention and care in a restaurant!

Nobody else does it!

- ---

- ---
- ---

- ---
- ---

- ---
- ---

- ---
- ---

4. **Write a list of partial compensations for clients who are not totally unhappy but aren't completely satisfied either** (because the food took longer than expected, your employees made some mistake in the order, etc.). Think what you can do to fix the problem and make the client very happy.

- ---
- ---

- ---

- ---

- ---

- ---

Once you are done and have it written down, create a Restaurant Policy Workbook and include your USP and all these scenarios and solutions.

5. Meet with your staff, let them know clearly and unequivocally about your policy, and make sure that they understand that not only will the restaurant lose revenue, but they may also lose their tips if the customers don't have to pay.

Unhappy clients are bad business for everybody!

Your staff must know that you mean business, and that the guests are the reason you are in business. They also need to focus a positive attitude towards the clients.

Your entire staff needs to strive hard to please your (their) clients, and to make their experience memorable.

Anything else is unacceptable.

Chapter 4:
Why You Must Have a
Strategic Mindset

You need to have a vision if you want to succeed

Most of your competitors - indeed most small business owners for that matter - are tactical. They care about how they run their restaurant on a daily basis. They worry about generating enough revenue to keep their business going. They worry about making the weekly or monthly payments, and making a profit after paying the bills. But sometimes they don't have a vision about where they want to go or how they want to grow their business.

In fact, they are so busy with the day-to-day operations that they don't spend time thinking about engineering a business approach that maximizes not only the revenue, but also their growth potential.

This is a big mistake.

You can't reach a target without knowing the target you are aiming at.

It is like driving a car without a destination. You may know how to drive the vehicle, how to fuel it and even how to fix the car in case it breaks, but if you don't know where you are going - if you don't have a road map or a destination - you'll just drive around aimlessly.

There are three components that are key to your success as a restaurateur and as a person: Vision, Strategy and Operations.

- **Vision:** What you want the organization to be (your dream).

- **Strategy:** What you are going to do to achieve your vision.

- **Operations:** What is the roadmap or how you will achieve your strategy.

Your vision is your dream of what you want your restaurant (or your life for that matter) to be. Your strategy is the large-scale plan you will follow to make the dream happen. Your operations are the specific actions you will take to follow the plan.

We will start with the vision and work down to the operations as we plan for your restaurant.

You need to always start with the vision statement (sometimes called a *mission statement*). When you know what the vision is, you can develop a strategy to get you to that vision. When you have decided on a strategy, you can improve your operations to meet the strategy.

Vision

A vision is an overriding idea of what your restaurant should be. It needs to reflect your dream. Your vision could be, for example, to be "the finest restaurant in the US", "the maker of the best pasta dishes in Boston", or "the best inexpensive quality food in town". You can also extend it to your entire life with a vision like: "I want to own the best restaurant in town and train my staff so that they can run it by themselves so I can have more free time to dedicate to my family".

A vision must be sufficiently clear and concise that everyone on your staff understands it and can buy into it with passion.

A vision - YOUR vision - can propel your restaurant from run-of-the-mill to greatness; it can change your positioning in the marketplace and differentiate your business from your competitors since most of them don't have a vision.

Now, there are two ways to create your Vision:

1. Create a new one from scratch.

2. Build one based on improving your existing business model.

I would encourage you to use the first approach. After all, a new vision is usually not evolutionary, but revolutionary. Don't assume that the old rules apply and don't let your current model dictate your vision.

If you already have a clear vision and you just want to improve upon it, then you can refine it or expand it. In this case perhaps the second option will work for you.

However, for the majority of restaurant owners, it is better to start with a clean slate. Dedicate some time when you have a quiet moment to thinking about your vision. (In the homework for this chapter, you'll find many questions that will help you to find your vision.)

The vision that you have will enable you to see exactly the sequence of events to incredible growth and success.

However, having a vision is very difficult if you don't have the process to get you there. You need to have a vision and believe in it, but you also need to lay down the path (strategy) to take you there.

You need to be different. You need to take some time and ask yourself the following question:

If you could accomplish anything that you dream of, what would that be?

The answer to this question will determine your own vision and the strategy to take you there. So, at the end, your strategy is the direction that you will take to reach your vision.

Let me repeat that:

"Your vision is whatever you want it to be."

It is something personal that fits your needs and your dreams. It is something that fulfills your motivation for accomplishment and inspires you, your staff, and your clients.

Some of the questions that you may ask yourself when determining your vision are:

- What do you want to accomplish with your business?

- How can you create value for your clients?

- What's your ultimate goal?

  o To have a very profitable restaurant where the staff and clients are happy?

  o To grow the business and expand by opening new restaurants?

  o To have the top restaurant in town?

  o To offer an exclusive and prize-winning menu?

  o What other factors do you want to include?

Although these questions look somewhat generic, they are important to ask so you understand where you want to take your business, and what your vision for your restaurant is.

We mentioned before that many restaurant owners spend the bulk of their time on the day-to-day operations: dealing with providers, staff, clients, accountants, banks, etc. without ever spending the time to sit down and think about their vision - their ultimate goal for owning the place.

Every step that you take towards your vision will get you closer to the goal.

We said before that strategy is what you will do with your restaurant to realize your vision. So let's now talk about your strategy, because you need a strategy if you want to accomplish your vision.

Strategy

Strategy is what you will do with your restaurant to realize your vision. It is made up of objectives to reach your goal, your destination. Creating a new Strategy or improving and changing your current one is the fastest, easiest and most powerful way to change your results and transform your operations.

To realize your Vision, you need a Strategy.

Strategy is the master purpose of your business and it is different from your business model. It is - or it should be - the explanation that supports the way that you operate your business.

You need a strategy to get where you want to go (a road map that will take you to your destination, your Vision). This strategy must be more than just desiring income or profit.

The most effective business strategy is the one that embodies the full spectrum of your life.

So how do you create a strategy to make your vision a reality?

First you need to understand that **you do have a strategy that you are currently following**, even if it's a reactive strategy and not a proactive one.

You need to think about how you will more effectively accomplish the activities in your business.

You need to learn what operating approach will provide you with the greatest outcome in the fastest time on a continuous basis. Your objective is always **optimization**.

This means that you need to get the greatest return from the least amount of time, energy and money at the lowest possible risk.

Ask yourself the following questions:

- What opportunities exist within my restaurant that I haven't yet exploited?

- What would be the benefit to my clients if I approach these opportunities?

- What would I need (additional capital, more employees, new facilities, etc.) to make this opportunity happen?

- Who else would benefit from my success if I were to introduce this new product/process/service?

    o Clients, distributors, etc?

- What are the missing pieces in my new strategy? Resources, money, actions, etc?

Answering these questions will help you determine your roadmap - your strategy.

For example: Let's assume that your current strategy is to bring the highest possible number of clients to your business. You probably spend money in coupons, ads (both in newspapers and magazines), Yellow Pages, etc. with the ultimate goal of increasing your customer base.

Now what happens if you change your mindset: **your ultimate strategy is not to increase the number of clients but to increase your profit margin and the money that you make**?

What about if, by giving free meals to loyal customers for special occasions (such as anniversaries and birthdays discussed in chapter 10), you could increase the frequency of visits, or the amount that their referrals - family, friends, coworkers - spend in your place?

What about if you set up a formalized referral system that will cost you nothing and bring ten times more people than your current coupons?

Do you see where I am going? Before you spend your money blindly, you need to have a strategy behind your actions.

Let's now work on creating your Strategy by following these steps:

1. Make a list of the highest-performing businesses that you know of. It doesn't matter

if they are outside the restaurant industry; in fact, many of them might be in other industries.

- What is their business strategy? What are they trying to accomplish?

- How do they operate to accomplish this strategy? (By the way, this is the difference between Strategy and Operations.)

2. **Look at the details of some of the strategies that you've identified from these companies, and then see how you can bring them to your own business.**

- Please, keep in mind that you can't create your own strategy until you don't understand or know your Vision.

- Your Strategy is the path that will take you to your destination: your Vision.

- Once you know that work backwards and write down what you need to do to get you to the Vision.

To accomplish this, let's do an exercise:

Close your eyes and imagine yourself three years from today arriving to your restaurant. Try to make the image as vivid as possible in your mind.

- What does your restaurant look like? Does it look like the one that you have today? Does it look different? If so, what's different about it?

- What about your employees? Do you picture in your mind having the same people or do you see different employees? If they are different, why aren't they the same people as now? Aren't you happy with the people that work at your place now?

- What about your clients? Do you see happy clients smiling and chatting over some great food and drinks? Do you see a more upscale clientele or your current customer type? (We will talk in detail about what kind of clients you want later on in this chapter since they are a key element in the success of your business.)

3. **Now, what's going to take to get from where you are today to this future that you just**

imagined?

- Imagine yourself, still in this near future, talking to a friend (or your spouse) and explaining how your place was two years ago and how it is now, explaining the changes that you needed to make to arrive at this point.

- So, if you want to accomplish your dream in two years, you obviously need to make some changes now (or at least soon).

- If operations continue as they do, you will still be as you are two years from now.

As you can see, we are now talking about your personal life as well as your business. This is because both are intrinsically interrelated. You can't have a strategy without taking into consideration both your personal and professional goals, since you are only one person with one life.

By the way, I found and followed a method that greatly helped me to define my vision and strategy. It is called Simple.ology (yes, with the weird period in the middle).

Simpleology proves that success and happiness are easier to achieve than most people think they are. In fact, people can almost guarantee their own success simply by following a few simple rules. These "5 Laws of Simpleology" aren't new; they've been around forever.

However, even though Simpleology has had more impact in my life than any other personal development program I have ever experienced, I do have to warn you that it will only work if you do what it asks. There is no such thing as a magic pill. Simpleology is boiled down to a short 15 minutes exercise that you perform every day. If you want the incredible changes in your mastery of Time, Energy, and Money, you must do the fun exercise every day. The changes aren't going to happen unless you do.

You can check for yourself and follow the first module called Simpleology 101 free of charge by going to their web site: http://www.simpleology.com/p/s101/joser/s101 and opening a free account. They will provide you with really good, fun and easy to follow lessons.

Operations

There are two questions that you must ask yourself to move towards your goal:

1. What keeps you busy every day?

2. What do you need to change (in your behavior, your planning, your life) to get you where you want to be?

A growing number of restaurateurs are increasingly frustrated with their life/work balance. Even if your business is doing okay, you need to increasingly sacrifice your personal life to run your business.

You spend more and more time keeping the train running: taking care of minor details and moving from one crisis to another.

If you stop for a moment and ask yourself about the specific things you accomplished last month - or even last week - you will probably be puzzled. You were very busy, for sure, extinguishing fires and managing priorities but did you accomplish anything meaningful that took you a step closer to your goal?

There is never a good time to get away from the day-to-day operations and reflect about your goals, your ambitions, and the reason you started or bought a business in the first place.

In the end it is not a matter of making lots of money; it is a matter of achieving freedom.

I think that the number one reason why businesses fail is due to a lack of strategic thinking and process improvements. We all only have 24 hours a day, from the poorest of the poor to the richest of the rich; nobody can buy or sell time.

The main difference between successful and unsuccessful people is what they do with these 24 hours.

In opinion polls in the United States and Europe, people complain more about the lack of time than the lack of money or freedom. Time is becoming more valuable than money.

You know the deal: sometimes you would take a well-deserved vacation but feel anxious about leaving somebody in charge to open and close your restaurant, because you were afraid that your business would suffer while you were away.

Here is the fundamental thought I want you to remember:

"If you keep on operating as you are doing at the present, you'll get the same results as you are getting now."

Read the previous sentence again and think about it.

If you don't change fundamentally - strategically - the way that you operate your business, you will get the same results that you are getting now. And you'll probably be feeling the same way you do now.

Now I assume that, if you are reading this book, you are not happy with the results that you are getting, or at the least you'd like to improve them in a substantial way. Otherwise you wouldn't be spending your time and money in this course.

Change is difficult. It causes stress, fear, and disrupts our habits, our usual way to operate. However, embracing change is the first step to freeing yourself from the daily routine that keeps you working aimlessly without a clear goal.

Strengths

Let's now talk about something directly related to your operations, strategy, and vision: **Your Strengths**.

In our western culture, we are constantly made aware of our deficiencies and flaws. We spend an incredible amount of time working on our weaknesses, and trying to learn about areas (such as setting up a home computer) that might not be interesting to us, and therefore areas where we are not very proficient.

As a result of this cultural behavior, we work really hard paying attention to our weaknesses, taking valuable time from promoting and moving forward with our strengths.

Instead, we should "manage" our weaknesses so that they don't interfere with our growth, but focus in and promoting our strengths so that we can be really successful in both our personal and professional lives.

So how can you determine your strengths? Donald O. Clifton and Paula Nelson outline in their book "Soar with Your Strengths " five clues to identifying your strengths:

- **Yearning:** Identify the kind of activities that you are naturally drawn to.

- **Quick Learning:** Identify the activities that you learn really fast.

- **Easy Flow:** In which activities did the steps come to you naturally or unconsciously?

- **Glimpses of excellence:** During what activities have you had moments of subconscious excellence where you were amazed of yourself?

- **Satisfaction:** What activities do you really enjoy doing?

Some scientists have researched for many years an area called "optimal performance". They came up with the theory that we all have two to three characteristics such as special skills or strengths: the more time that we spend developing these areas, the greater the chance for us to be successful.

Let's do an exercise to help you identifying and implementing the strengths theory.

Use the next page (you can make copies if you want to keep it for the future) and write down your top three priorities or responsibilities as a restaurant owner as #1, #2 and #3.

Below those priorities write (on the a, b & c lines) the daily activities and tasks that help you make progress, and get you closer to your top priorities. Think about the tasks needed to accomplish the top three priorities that you listed.

What do you need to do every day to move in the direction to accomplish these tasks?

Now go back and rank each individual task, beginning with the ones that are most enjoyable and natural to you. I want you to focus on which tasks you really enjoy doing.

Go through the list and place an **A** next to the tasks that you are excellent at and that you enjoy doing.

Review the list again and rank with a **B** the tasks that you are good at and that you don't mind doing.

Now rank with a **C** the tasks that you are just competent at and that you really don't enjoy doing.

Finally rank with **D** or **F** the tasks that you struggle with and that you really dislike.

Review one last time the list and make sure that all the tasks are ranked.

Now starting from the bottom of the ranking, look at the **Fs** (or **Ds** if you're using them) and think about who can do this task better than you? It could be an internal employee or perhaps you need to outsource it to an external vendor or partner. This is called *"Managing your weaknesses"*.

For example, you may hate bookkeeping but this is an activity that must be done. You can outsource this to your CPA or a professional bookkeeper. The extra cost will be totally worth it in the time and energy that you save not doing it yourself (and don't forget: we expend a lot of bad energy trying to do things that we hate or just don't like).

Or perhaps you hate dealing with statistics and numbers but you still need to know what dishes sell best and which ones give you the most profit margin, etc.

You can find an employee who is really good at detail-oriented tasks or organizing and analyzing information, and pay him/her some extra money to do this job for you. Of course you will ultimately make the strategic decisions about your menus, pricing, etc., but somebody else can do the actual compiling and putting together the information in a clear and understandable way.

It may be that you have employees that are really good at some of the tasks that you hate. If this is the case, assign those tasks to those employees. They will be grateful to you for receiving a task that they love, and will do it for recognition or a small amount of money.

Make sure that you choose a person with excellent skills and/or passion for the tasks that you are delegating. If he or she has a desire to do the task, you can train the employee if he or she doesn't have the skills yet to perform the task.

Do not try to dump things on people just because they are available or because you want to avoid the tasks.

You need to look for somebody who can perform the task at an **A** level (or at least a **B**). If you don't have anybody in-house, outsource it to an external partner. You can even suggest bartering or trading food for services. We will talk about bartering in the next Chapter (Chapter 5).

Move now to the **C**s, then do the same for the As and Bs if you want to have an alternate person be able to perform the tasks.

Your goal is to delegate all the tasks that you are neither exceptional nor excellent at (that is, all the tasks that are not aligned with your strengths).

If you see that you already have several **A** tasks, try to delegate some of the **B**s as well. Although you may be good at them, we are striving for excellence here.

I want you to spend most of your time on your main strengths. Not only will you be much happier, but you'll also increase **dramatically** the performance of your business.

Your Priorities

1. _____

    a. _____

    b. _____

    c. _____

2. _____

    a. _____

    b. _____

    c. _____

3. _____

    a. _____

    b. _____

    c. _____

What kind of clients do you want?

This looks like a silly question at first: Obviously you want great clients!

However, this question is very important, as you will soon see. You need to know what kind of clients are you looking for before you spend your hard earned marketing dollars.

This is another strategic decision that you need to make:

You need to define your target market if you want to succeed.

A target market is characterized by age, sex, geography and economic classification. Before you can set out to launch your marketing campaign, you need to identify the market to which your restaurant would best serve.

For example, do you have a high-end restaurant? If so, you should focus on affluent people who can afford your prices, who don't mind spending some extra dollars to get the best food, service and ambience that you can deliver. These people would probably be comprised of middle-age individuals or couples with grownup kids, successful professionals or entrepreneurs, etc.

Or perhaps you prefer to cater to families. In this case, your audience will be younger couples with kids, with lower spending power who are looking for a kids-friendly restaurant where they can still enjoy good food (versus fast food chains).

Do you see the concept of market segmentation?

Market Segmentation is the process of dividing a market (or client types) into defined groups with similar needs or comparable behavior and attitudes. This would increase the probability of an appropriate response to a marketing initiative such as an advertisement campaign.

The shortest route to failure would be trying to be a jack-of-all-trades spending your dollars trying to market to different unrelated people.

People without children (or couples having a "date night" without the kids) might be looking for a high class, romantic or chic restaurant; they won't be very happy having screaming children seating next to them.

On the other hand, families with kids would feel very uncomfortable in a formal ambience with soft music and elegantly dressed people.

SOME GUIDELINES TO HELP YOU UNDERSTAND HOW TO TARGET YOUR CLIENTELE:

1. **Each group must be independently large enough to be profitable:** To achieve any economy of scale the size of the audience needs to be considered.

   For example, you wouldn't want to target your marketing to Chiropractors in your area if you only have 3 practitioners with offices nearby.

2. **Each group must be easily accessible:** You don't want to spend your marketing dollars on a national TV ad or a local magazine in a different state, because 99% of your clients will be living nearby (you may attract a few travelers, but this would be a high price to pay for a very small return on your investment!)

3. **You need to market your restaurant through media that resonates with this group:** It doesn't make sense to market to a group of people that is not interested in your place. For example, you don't want to advertise in a weekly magazine whose main audience is college students and Indy music if you have a high-end restaurant. Most of them won't be able to afford a dinner in your place anyway so this is a waste of money.

http://www.myrestaurantmarketing.com

4. **The purchasing power of the group must be measurable:** To position your restaurant and price your menus effectively, it is very useful to know the purchasing power of the group that you are targeting. Of course, there are some obvious clients with money such as lawyers, architects, doctors, judges, small business owners, etc. but some other segments may not be as obvious.

5. If you want to expand your clientele base, you need to do some research about these new groups that you want to target before you spend your marketing budget.

So I hope that it's clear that market segmentation (or clientele grouping) is the start point for the launch of any marketing initiative, and will direct the strategic decisions you make.

Although all of this may sound complicated, actually it is not. It all boils down to having a very clear vision about what kind of clients you want to target.

The more specific that you can get in selecting the group of people that will constitute your main clientele base, the more successful that you will be with your marketing campaigns. Keep in mind the point number 1 that we mentioned in the segmentation rules: **Each group must be independently large enough to be profitable.**

On one hand, you don't want to be so specific that you limit your clients; on the other hand, you don't want to market to all audiences as we mentioned before.

If you target a large enough segment, while maintaining your focus (look at similarities between different professions: for example, education levels, income-earning ability, networking opportunities, etc.), you can then use your marketing tools efficiently and move way ahead of your competitors.

Personally, I dislike marketing tools such as the Yellow Pages, newspapers, radio and TV ads, because you can't target your segment (audience). In these marketing vehicles the criteria to display your ad could be as simple as where the name of your business falls in the alphabet or if the size of your ad fits nicely in the newspaper or magazine page layout, regardless of how you compare to other restaurants that could appeal to your target audience.

If you can identify a substantial, yet focused niche segment, you can immediately gain a competitive advantage since you can customize and target some events in your place specifically for that market.

For example, you could host "Doctors Lunches or Dinners" where doctors can go to your place because they can meet peers, and perhaps do some networking. You could do the same thing with Lawyers, CPAs, etc.

You see where I'm going?

In the next two chapters, we'll talk about Leverage and explain Bartering Techniques.

These are very important concepts, and will be very powerful tools that will help show you how you can maximize your profits and investments *"leveraging"* the tools and services that you already have available.

Don't forget to do your homework!

H O M E W O R K

The homework for this Chapter is essential for you to come up with your Vision and realize your Strategy.

I've compiled a series of questions that will make you think strategically instead of tactically.

Please don't overlook the importance of answering these questions. Even if you think that they are not related to your current business or your particular issues and problems, they will help you to understand that you may be doing things that don't really matter or that you are putting your efforts in the wrong issues.

These questions will help you focus and concentrate your energy on the things that matter the most for you, your family and your business.

Now it's time to work. Get a piece of paper and write down the answer to the following questions:

Vision

- What's your ultimate goal and vision for your restaurant?

- What vision, purpose and values are currently present in your restaurant?

- What vision, purpose and values would you like to change or improve?

- What new vision, purpose and/or values would you like to create?

- What steps do you need to take - starting today - to realize your vision?

- What meaningful difference(s) will you make in your business if you can accomplish your vision? How could the difference(s) affect your community?

- How do you want to affect the lives of your employees, your providers, your clients, and your family?

- If you could do absolutely anything that you wanted in the restaurant industry, what would that be?

- What's keeping you for not doing it?

- In your wildest dreams, what would you like people to say about your restaurant or about you?

- What's your vision for the next five years?

- Are you moving towards that vision? If not, why not?

Strategy

- If you were a customer dining in your own restaurant, what would you change? Why?

- What are the three major changes that you think will affect the restaurant industry in the next five to ten years?

- What do you need to do to participate in those changes?

- What's the most important thing that you offer to your clients?

- Why is that important to you?

- Why do you think is that important to them?

- What do you need to do/improve/change so that your clients are really happy with their dinning experience at your place?

- What do other restaurants offer that people really like (you can check positive reviews of your competitors in places like www.Citysearch.com, www.restaurant.com, www.zagat.com or www.yelp.com)?

- Would you like to offer the same elements of your successful competitors? What's holding you back from offering them? What can you do to fix this?

- Look at other industries (not directly related with the food or beverage industry) and think what could you learn from some of their techniques/processes/marketing?

- What products do other companies (non-competitors) offer that you could offer to your clients?

- What are the most obvious weaknesses of your restaurant?

- What steps are you implementing to address these weaknesses?

- If you were opening your restaurant again from scratch, what would you do differently?

- What other products could you offer to increase your sales? (We will talk about this point in much more detail in Chapter 9, but I want you to start thinking about it now).

Chapter 5:
Leverage

Maximize your Efforts

Leverage in the broadest sense is an assisted advantage. As a verb, to use leverage means to gain an advantage through the use of a tool. For example, you can more easily lift a heavy object with a lever than by lifting it unaided.

The term leverage is commonly used in a metaphorical sense. As a frequently used business or marketing term, leverage means any strategic or tactical advantage. Business executives sometimes use it as a means to exploit an opportunity, just as the use of a physical lever gives one an advantage when moving or lifting an object to a new location.

The concept of leverage is critical to the success of your restaurant.

So let's assume that you are determined to increase the number of your clients.

You could try to talk one-on-one with many of your patrons, or you could create a marketing campaign that will reach thousands at a time. An effective campaign is a tool, using this tool will give us an advantage. It will give us leverage.

If you can reach existing or potential clients thousands at a time at very little or no cost, you will leverage your efforts and be marketing in a superb way.

Operations and Employees Leverage

These are some examples of leverage applied to your operations and employees:

1. Attracting the best workers available in your area, happy and motivated to work for you.

2. Training programs for your employees that multiply their effectiveness.

3. Improving your workflow and processes so that there is a consistent, efficient way of doing things. You need to make sure that everybody is clear about their roles and responsibilities, and there is not

overlapping, miscommunication or delays because your processes are not clear, defined and understood by all your employees.

4. Your leadership - the greatest source of people leverage - that supports and encourages the staff, which multiplies the efforts of and magnifies the results from your entire team

5. Sharing your Vision, Purpose, Values and Strategy with your employees, distributors and clients.

You need to optimize your people and processes until you become a well-oiled restaurant sales machine. The best way to do this is to create an Employee Training Program. Here is how to do it:

EMPLOYEE TRAINING PROGRAM STEP BY STEP

If you don't have it yet, start writing a training program for your employees.

Although this can sound overwhelming, you don't need to write a 600-page training book. These are some steps that you can take that will help you write your Training Program in no time:

1. Buy a 3 ring binder and add a cover saying: **Employee Training Program** in big bold letters.

2. Write down the following sections:

   a. Vision

   b. Goals

   c. Strategy

   d. USP

   Now enter your vision, your goals for the restaurant, your Unique Selling Proposition (USP) and your Strategy, so that all your employees know and are clear about it.

3. Write down one new section and call it OPERATIONS

4. Within the Operations section, list the basic things that you want them to do. Some things that you can cover are:

   • Cash management policy

   • Opening and Closing of the restaurant checklist

   • Roles and Responsibilities

- Policies to compensate a disgruntled or unhappy client

- Tips management and payment

- Vacations, rotation and schedules

- Etc.

You can keep on adding to this manual every time that you see gaps or processes that are not clear.

The beauty of having written policies is that every time you hire new employees they can quickly absorb the principles and values that your restaurant has.

Written policies also help your existing employees to be clear about their roles and responsibilities, as well as how to communicate your values and USP to your clients, and explains how to react when something is not working fine.

Once you have this manual completed, make sure that all new and existing employees read it and use it often as a reference. Make copies for each employee, and keep a copy in the restaurant that's available for them to look at in case that there is any confusion or issue.

Sales and Marketing Leverage

These are some examples of leverage applied to your sales and marketing:

1. Marketing programs that leverage your USP as discussed in the previous chapters.

2. Active involvement and participation in your local Chamber of Commerce, or any other professional networking group where you can leverage your name and reputation.

3. Creating an incredible experience for your clients.

4. Lowering the cost of your menus while maintaining their quality.

5. Creating strategic partnerships with other businesses or professionals. (We'll talk about this one later since it is very important for increasing your bottom line and the number of clients that you can bring to your place).

6. Anticipating the future (based on your Strategic Planning and Vision covered in Chapter 4) so that you can start implementing some steps that will take you there.

These are all examples of using tools that will give you an advantage against your competitors in the restaurant business.

Test Your Marketing

A key aspect to using leverage in your business and growing it exponentially is testing. You can't know if the marketing tools you are using are the right ones - or if you are using them the right way - unless you test them.

Anyone can become a marketing genius by doing one simple thing: Testing the different marketing strategies and comparing them to see which one gives us the most return for our investment.

When you use safe, small tests you'll eliminate costly expenses, reducing your risk and quickly promoting what works. We've already mentioned using your data to see which menu dishes work and which ones don't, and we can also apply testing to our marketing campaigns.

It is amazing to me how few restaurant owners even bother to test their marketing strategies, wasting thousands of dollars in the process.

http://www.myrestaurantmarketing.com

Many restaurateurs spend money based upon whatever the marketing pro or advertising rep who happens to stop by their place advises them to do, and often don't even bother to measure if these marketing investments bring enough clients to their place to justify their expense.

They bet their dollars on arbitrary and subjective decisions, instead of trying to come up with a proven system that gives them the best return for their investments.

When you look at your marketing efforts, the one thing that you MUST do is always test your marketing to make sure that you are maximizing your sales results.

You must always probe for customer response since - for the same amount of money - you can leverage your results a hundredfold or more if you test different marketing strategies.

For example, if you post two different coupons in the same advertising campaign, you will most likely see that one of them pulls much better than the other.

It could be the same offer geared to the same target audience. However, the wording in one of them could make a huge difference in the response that it gets.

Many times, we don't know why this happens, we just know that it does and we should analyze the results.

Your job is to figure out what made one of the coupons work so much better than the other:

- Was an action that you ask the readers to take more effective than another one?

- Were the words that you used in your headlines different?

- Were the coupons published on different days?

Any one of these variables could have an impact on the results that you get from your advertising. Your job is to analyze each one and distill down the key component (or components) that worked for you.

Once you identify this component (after your analysis tells you which offer, headline and text worked best - and brought you the highest number of clients), then your job is to improve upon it.

You need to test and retest your ads (in each medium you choose to use). Continuous improvement in your advertising is the best and most inexpensive way to leverage your marketing.

Compare all your ads, sales letters, promotions, offers or discounts that you produced in the last months (or years if you are brave enough), and see which ones produced the best results.

By using the marketing that worked best, you will increase the efficiency of your marketing budget and lower your marketing and selling expenses.

So roll up your sleeves and test one price against another, one ad against another, one coupon against another and one promotion against another. Test your current offer or your new satisfaction guarantee or your preferred client program... you get the point.

There are many variables in each marketing program and you need to test all of them until you reach the perfect combination that will make your marketing the most leveraged and effective that there is.

A very important factor to test is the price of your dishes. Higher is not always better since many times by lowering a dish a few dollars, you can increase the sales exponentially.

Let your clients tell you the correct price. Do not try to guess it.

You first need to know the cost of each of your dishes, and the profit margins that you are getting from each of them. Different prices for the same dish could propel sales of that dish beyond current levels. The best way to test the prices is to offer special promotions.

Let's say that one item on your menu is Grilled Halibut with herbs, etc., and you regularly sell it at $28. Your cost on this dish is $16, so you are making a profit of $12 (43% of the total price) every time that you sell this particular dish.

To test this price point, first gather information about how many dishes you sell on daily, weekly and monthly bases. Determine the average based on the last 6 to 12 months (or whatever information you can get from your computer). Now, raise the price for three months to $32 - for a total gain of $16 each time that you sell the dish.

Your profit margin is now 50%. Your price is now double your cost; instead of the 43% that you previously received every time that you sell a halibut dish, you now get an additional four dollars per dish.

After three months, look at your sales figures and check how many dishes you've sold. Did you sell as many as before?

To make a fair comparison, it would be great if you could compare similar months in previous years. We all know that the restaurant business is very seasonal, so we need to take this variable out of the equation.

Did you sell more? (You may be surprised to find out that sometimes an increase in the price can bring *additional* sales of that dish.) Did you sell less? If you sold less, did you still make the same gross revenue as when the price was lower?

This exercise will give you an excellent view of how sensitive your clients are to the price of your dishes. (This is called "elasticity" in economics.)

Now, let's do the reverse. For the following next three months lower the price of your halibut dish down to $24. Now your profit is $8 per dish (or 33%).

Let's illustrate this with a graphic:

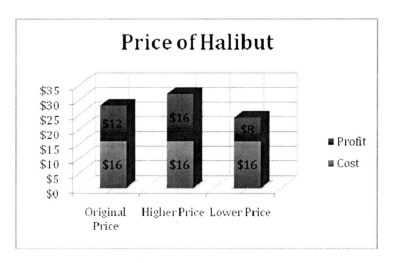

Again, make a comparison of sales and profits. Compare your results with the sales and profits of the original (sold at $28) and increased price (sold at $32)

Were the sales better or worse than with the original price? Better or worse than with the increased price?

You can see clearly which one worked the best for you.

This exercise takes guessing out of the equation. It gives you a powerful tool to price your dish (and do the same with the rest of your menu - one or two dishes at a time) until you find the perfect balance between price and profitability.

And, of course, you can always raise the prices after a while and check again!

With this testing, your clients will tell you what price is the right one for each dish; you don't have to guess it!

If a regular customer notices the changes and asks you about the price differences, you can always say that you are adapting the prices to the market conditions. They will see higher prices sometimes and lower some other times, and they should be okay with this explanation.

Once you are done with all your menu dishes, use this technique with new dishes before adding them into your printed menu. You could offer them as the special of the week, or the month, etc. In this way you know early on that the prices that you are asking are the right ones for your clients.

Remember, this is the **only** way to clearly find the "right" price for your menu. You will be amazed at the differences in profit and number of dishes served that one price can bring versus another. Just a few dollars higher or lower can be the disparity between mediocre and excellent sales.

Here we saw a specific example of menu prices testing. Of course, you can test other leveraging tools using similar techniques. You could test different training programs for your employees, different methods for recruiting people, different vendors, your daily processes, your marketing campaigns, etc.

You get the point.

By applying tests to all your leveraging tools you can dramatically improve your results, since you'll know that you are always doing the right thing and not trying to guess. The results of your testing will always tell you what you need to know: how to implement the correct strategy each and every time.

Other Leveraging Possibilities

Restaurants are interesting businesses. They have lots of assets and therefore lots of possibilities to leverage these assets.

Think about the assets that you have in your restaurant. You can divide your assets in two different categories:

1. Your Material Assets such as your place, inventory, etc.

2. Your Staff's Skills

3. Your Providers, Distributors, other professionals, etc.

4. Your Clients

Now you need to think how you can profit from these assets. Let's look at each one in a little more detail:

LEVERAGING YOUR MATERIAL ASSETS

1. One obvious asset that you have is your place. You've put lots of effort and money to make your restaurant beautiful so that people go there to have a meal in an inviting atmosphere.

   So what are you doing with your beautiful place when you are not open for business, or even when your business is slow? Probably not much.

   Now think, how could you leverage your place so that you can get some profit from it? One way would be to think about who needs a gathering place (like a restaurant) to conduct business?

Think: hotels.

Who books conference rooms in hotels? I can think of many possibilities:

- Professional Associations

- Seminar Presenters

- Public Speakers

- Corporate Events

- Etc.

Now, what does a hotel conference room has that is needed to host seminars, conferences and other business meetings?

Let's see:

- Internet access

- Wireless connection

- Tables and chairs

- A screen and a projector (actually they don't always provide with this, most of the time they charge additional fees to rent one)

- A stereo system

- Catering services

- Privacy

Wow, guess what? You've already got most of these necessities!

Your restaurant probably already has Internet access; and if not, it is very easy to get it installed by calling your cable or phone company and requesting high-speed Internet access. You should expect to pay around $50 to $70 a month for the high-speed Internet subscription.

Once you have internet access, you only need to buy a wireless router (very inexpensive) and – voila - you've got wireless access for your clients, and a way to get extra business. You can ask one of your employees to set it up for you (if they have technical skills) or hire somebody to do it. It shouldn't take more than half an hour of their time.

What else? Let's see: you've already got tables, chairs, probably a stereo system (since most likely you have ambience music), food (of course) and you could close your restaurant at lunch time and give total privacy to the party.

The only thing that you are missing might be a projector and a screen. You can buy these for around $2,000 together, a worthwhile investment if you start doing this type of business.

You see where I'm going? You could use slow lunch days to create a conference room in your place. And you should advertise with your local Chamber of Commerce or trade magazines aimed at the professionals you want to attract.

You can also check: http://www.allconferences.com/ . This is how they market themselves: "It is a directory focusing on conferences, conventions, trade shows, exhibits, workshops, events and business meetings. This is a unique search directory that serves users looking for specific information on conference or event information while at the same time provides services to the meeting planners, such as online registrations and payment processing."

Then there are sites targeted to meeting planners such as: http://www.mpiweb.org/cms/mpiweb/default.aspx where you can list your place. Just search for meeting planners + your city or state, and you'll find lots of information that you can use to contact local planners and let them know about your new "meeting place".

By the way, you can make money two ways hosting these kinds of events:

1. They will pay you for renting your place

2. You can cater to them

To determine how much to charge, just call some hotels around your area and ask how much their fees are for hosting events in their conference rooms. Estimate how many people you can fit comfortably in your place and make your request based on that figure.

You'll likely need to re-arrange tables, etc. to adapt to the needs of the meeting planners, but this is a small amount of work.

LEVERAGING YOUR STAFF'S SKILLS

Your employees probably have skills that you don't even know about. Do you have people that are technically savvy? What about artistic or design skills? Do they play any instruments? Do they have any hobbies or skills that you can leverage?

You see, many times you might spend money outside when you have the solution in front of your nose, and you may never have considered using your own people.

For example, if one of your employees is really good with computers you can ask him or her to setup your wireless connection or they can assist with troubleshooting and other tasks or even to create a database to keep track of your clients (I will talk more about this in detail in Chapter 10).

The same idea applies to designing needs. They can help you design your web site, your menus, your stationary, etc.

Of course, you should compensate your employees for any extra task that they perform at your place. If you ask them to do specialized work for the minimum salary (remember, they won't get tips for these tasks), they will resent you and probably refuse to help you.

Just give them a bonus or pay them extra hours or give them some paid free time and they will do their best to help you out.

LEVERAGING YOUR PROVIDERS, DISTRIBUTORS, AND OTHER PROFESSIONALS

You are surrounded by all kinds of people with various skills, and everybody is willing to try to make an extra buck, so why don't you use their skills to accomplish tasks that you can't do on your own?

Delegation is perhaps one of the most underused and underestimated techniques. If there are people who can do things better than you, don't waste your time struggling with those tasks, focus on your strengths and delegate challenging tasks to somebody else.

Again, what kind of skills do the professionals that you interact with every day have that you can use? Can you add a new line of business to your restaurant by getting new products or services from them?

For example, you could make a deal with one of your distributors to display and sell some of their exclusive products in your place. You could then split the profits 50/50.

Or you could make a deal with your wine sales representatives to host a special wine tasting at your place.

What about making a deal with your carpet cleaner so that you can give discount coupons to your clients to clean their carpets in exchange for a free restaurant carpet cleaning?

The possibilities are endless, you just need to know the skills and areas of expertise of the people who serve in and provide to your restaurant - and use your imagination.

LEVERAGING YOUR CLIENTS

Your clients cover a wide rainbow of professions and skills that you can tap into.

You can network with your best clients, learn from them, know what they do, what are their professions, their skills, etc. and use these skills to improve your business.

For example, we talked about using slow lunch days to create conference centers in your restaurant. Why don't you bounce the idea to some of your clients who happen to organize seminars and conferences?

Not only you will get good feedback and ideas from them, but you will plant a seed in their minds so the next time that they (or somebody they work with or know personally) plan on organizing a conference or seminar, they will think of your place to host the event.

Likewise, you can hire some of your clients as attorneys, interior designers, CPAs, consultants, etc. to help you improve your business.

Perhaps, you can trade some of their services for money plus gift certificates. After all, they like your place and come often, don't they? So they probably won't refuse your gift certificates.

These are just a few of the many possibilities to leverage your assets. You need to always look for new opportunities to use what you've already got and try to maximize all your potential.

In the next chapter, I'll cover one of the most important leverage techniques that you can use: Bartering.

H O M E W O R K

This is the homework for this chapter:

EMPLOYEES & OPERATIONS

1. Meet with all your employees and discuss their roles and responsibilities.

2. Write down all the information and make sure that there are not gaps, and that there is no overlap or potential for miscommunication or delays because your processes are not clear, defined and understood by all your employees.

3. Share your Vision, Purpose, Values and Strategy with your employees, distributors and clients.

4. Start writing your **Employee Training Program**.

5. Ask your employees to review the program draft, and help you fill in gaps by giving you ideas, suggestions, etc.

SALES & MARKETING

1. Make a list of assets that you have in your restaurant. Create three categories:

   • Inventory, including your place. You don't need to go into detail, just list total assets.

   • Employee skills. Include hobbies, education and anything that could be helpful for your business. You'll be surprised to discover new skills and talents that you never knew about.

   • Food providers and other professionals that you interact with on a daily bases. List skills, responsibilities, etc. Again, look for possibilities of working together.

2. Look at the list and think how you can profit from these assets.

   • Is there any new business that you can generate with your current inventory or place? I mentioned previously about offering your place for seminars and conferences but there could be more possibilities, just be creative.

   • Do your employees have any skills that can help you delegate some of your tasks? Computer skills, designing skills, focus on detail, whatever they are good at that can be helpful.

- What about your providers? Can you use their skills, their professional knowledge, experience or contacts to do something together?

- Think about your clients. Do you know any who can help you with your business needs? Perhaps they can be a great source of networking or referrals?

Just keep an open mind and open eyes, and soon you will be discovering many new potential opportunities for leveraging your assets.

Chapter 6:
Bartering

How to Get Goods or Services Without Using Money

Let's talk now in detail about one of the most important leverage techniques that you can use: Bartering.

The dictionary defines bartering as: *"The action or system of exchanging goods or services without using money."*

You can exchange goods or services that you may need for something that you can offer. This is a really powerful mechanism to leverage your assets.

Bartering allows you to do things that you couldn't do otherwise on a tight budget – to obtain things you couldn't normally buy if you're short on cash or if you don't have unlimited buying power.

Perhaps you are not aware of it, but you have an excellent asset to trade: the dining experience you offer. Think about it. Everybody loves a good restaurant, and this means that you will be able to trade dining at your place for services that you may need - such as advertising, cleaning services, etc.

You can barter with many businesses. Not all businesses are constantly using 100% of their capacity or resources. They are often waiting for more work, so perhaps they could use gift certificates from your restaurant to give to their customers, or to invite patrons or benefactors to lunches or dinners, etc.

Let's elaborate on the concept of "exchanging dining for goods or services": You could approach a local business and let them know that you want to exchange their goods or services for gift certificates valid anytime at your restaurant (as good as cash).

For example, let's assume that you need $5,000 in some kind of services. You could offer 50 gift certificates at a value of $100 each in trade. Each business would be receiving comparable value; however, it might be much better for you if you persuade the business owner to accept 200 gift certificates for $25 value each.

The reason for this is that it they will have more gift certificates to distribute or use and it is likely that they will give them to more people, potentially bringing your restaurant many new potential clients. Besides, $25 in a fancy restaurant doesn't usually even pay for the whole meal - so it is likely that you can make some additional sales on wine, dessert, etc.

Many of these people will also likely bring their spouses, friends or colleagues with them, increasing your revenue. Also, sometimes they will lose the certificates or forget about them, so this is extra money that you could save on the barter exchange.

Let's assume that your cost in food is 1/3 of the total retail price of your dishes. So this $5,000 may cost you only around $1,600 in food. Of course this may vary for your restaurant, but for sure your cost is less than the selling price. If not, something is terribly wrong with your pricing!

Not only can you get services without spending upfront dollars for them, but you can also get many potential new clients by paying only 1/3 of the amount that you get in return.

Does this sound like a good deal to you? It should - because it is.

The important thing is that you can leverage your food cost to pay for services that you need.

As long as you have clients willing to eat at your place, you've got the basis for building a profitable barter opportunity.

This is a good moment for you to make up a list of all the goods or services you need or want for both your business and/or your home.

You may need new office equipment: computers, a fax machine. Or perhaps you need some plumbing work, a new dishwasher or refrigerator or equipment maintenance, electrical repairs, some other new appliances, such as an air conditioner or heating unit, etc.

You can check (or ask your accountant to check) the previous year's expenses. In this way you'll know in what categories you expended money and can identify the best candidates for bartering.

Once you've determined exactly what you need, you're ready to begin bartering – and profiting.

There are two main kinds of bartering: One-to-One bartering and Triangulation bartering. Let's look at them both in more detail.

One to One Bartering

Previously, we were referring to One to One Bartering. It is a direct exchange of your goods and services for other goods and services that you need or want.

Let's say you're trying to get your dishwasher serviced.

Go through the phone book and call every maintenance company that maintains industrial dishwashers in your area. The Yellow Pages are a really great resource for this task!

Introduce yourself and your business. Tell the owner of the business that you need a monthly service of your dishwasher, or perhaps a one-time service call (whatever works for you).

Tell the business owner that you'd like to trade an equal dollar amount of gift certificates for the amount of service you need. Be sure to stress that you seek to trade on retail value and not a discounted price that the service company may offer via coupons, etc. to some of their clients.

Dealing on a retail or suggested retail basis is an excellent way to effect most trades because the business owner will immediately see the advantage of selling their services for a full price on the transaction.

If, for example, the regular bill for servicing your dishwasher was $1,000 for a whole year, then you will trade $1,000 worth of gift certificates with him.

Whether he needs the gift certificates right now really doesn't matter, as long as he is persuaded that he'll be able to use these items or services immediately or in the near future. Whenever you require something right now, and the person or company you are trying to trade with doesn't need or want your gift certificates right away, don't let the deal slip away.

Offer the prospective trader the following options to sell him more effectively the idea of bartering with you:

1. Tell him he can have an unlimited expiration on the gift certificates.

2. Tell him that he may give them to his friends, family members or his best customers.

3. Ask him if he, his friends, customers and/or his family will spend $1,000 dining out in the next few months or years. Show him how these gift certificates will save them money. Remember he can use them for several years; there is no time limit!

4. Tell him you understand that sometimes business may be slower, and that you're willing to receive his services at that time.

Now you have created rational and persuasive reasons for him to exchange with you. If he understands he can "buy" this dining experience -

which he can also share - in exchange for his time (perhaps even doing it when his business is slower) he probably will jump at that chance.

The creative possibilities of such an approach are virtually limitless.

As I said, never try to trade your gift certificates at anything less than their retail value. Remember, the higher the valuation of your gift certificates, the greater the buying advantage that you get.

And by the way, you can also trade your gift certificates in exchange for other gift certificates from the business that you are bartering with. Just make sure that you have the same rights of use that they have:

1. No time limit, or at least several years' expiration.

2. Possibility of reassigning or giving the gift certificates or services to be performed to another party (family members, friends or customers).

This last point is very important. The owner of the business that you are bartering with has the opportunity to assign (give) your gift certificates to any 3rd party of their choice. You should also request from the business owner the flexibility of giving the gift certificates (or the services) that you've got from the bartering, to a third party of your choice.

Insist on the freedom to assign to somebody else any item or service you ever receive a credit for, so that somebody else can use it. This is very important to allow us to do Triangulation Bartering, as we will see next.

This is a graphic representation of the One on One Bartering:

Triangulation Bartering

Perhaps the single most valuable technique for the creative barterer to master is the fine art of triangulation bartering.

By becoming proficient at triangulation, you can make many more barter deals and achieve much higher net profits than the traditional trade deals produce.

Triangulation is the use of three or more separate transactions to achieve your ultimate barter objective. While it may seem complex in theory, it is really simple in practice. By the way, even if there are more than three transactions, we will still call it triangulation instead of some other funny names.

Triangulation becomes essential whenever you cannot achieve your primary barter objective through the conventional one-on-one bartering. In other words, whenever you cannot convince a barter prospect to accept your gift certificates directly for his goods, services or gift certificates, triangulation could help you save the deal.

Let's say that you need to print menus, marketing materials, business cards and your monthly newsletter. You go to your favorite printer and talk to the owner. You tell her what you want and she tells you that all these services will cost you $5,000.

Now, being the smart person that you are, you remember this book and decide to offer the owner gift certificates in exchange for her services.

T R A D I T I O N A L   O N E   O N   O N E   B A R T E R I N G

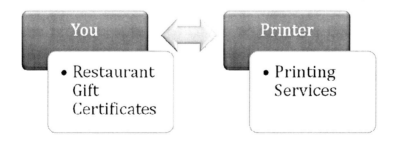

However, the owner of the printer doesn't need $5,000 in gift certificates because her clientele is small - or for any other reason.

What can you do in this situation? You probably could approach other printers who may also turn you down.

Or you can be creative and try the Triangular Bartering approach instead!

Let's use the previous assumption that $5,000 in gift certificates will really cost you $1,600 in food and beverages, and you'd like to trade gift certificates for the printing materials that you need for your restaurant.

Stop for a moment and analyze the print shop owner's profit-or-loss perspective. What goods or services does she need for her business? One possibility (and there are more -just be creative) could be advertising.

Most retail businesses spend between $5,000 and $10,000 a month on radio, TV and newspaper ads. How can you use advertising to help you trade credits at your restaurant for printing goods?

The answer is: through triangulation, of course.

Let's assume that the print shop owner needs to spend some money in advertising services. Instead of exchanging your restaurant gift certificates for her printing services, you will try to implement a triangulation bartering with the printing owner and the radio station as follows:

Exchanging your gift certificates with the radio station for advertising services

Exchanging these advertising services with the printing company for printing services that you'll use.

TRIANGULATION BARTERING STEP BY STEP

This is how it's done:

1. Approach all of the prominent radio and television stations in your area, plus the local newspapers and/or magazines.

2. Offer to provide them with restaurant credits they can use to "wine and dine" their best clients in exchange for advertising credits.

3. Request the right to assign the advertising credits to another party.

This is very important. You must obtain the rights to assign the advertising credits to a third party of your choice or you won't be able to use them for triangulation bartering.

TRIANGULATION
BARTERING

Let's look at the dollar amounts.

You trade $10,000 worth of your restaurant gift certificates for advertising services. These gift certificates can be used as the station sees fit –with no expiration date– for $10,000 worth of advertising services, with the provision that you can assign your newly acquired advertising credits at any time.

Now, it is possible that some stations would refuse your offer if they have plenty of advertisers paying for their air space or ad sections; but more often than not, you will find a local radio station or publication that will take your offer.

Then - with $10,000 worth of advertising in hand - you go back to the print shop owner. But now you have a different barter proposition. You no longer offer your gift certificates that they don't need. Now you'll offer advertising services in exchange for their printing services.

You still need $5,000 worth of printing services, and you now have $10,000 worth of advertising services. How should you make a deal with the print shop owner?

In the restaurant business (as we mentioned before) your cost is usually 1/3 of your sales price. You may pay $1,600 for food, converting it into meals selling for $5,000, making a profit of $3,400.

In the retail business, such as the printing services that you need, the cost of business is about 2/3 of the sales price. So if the printing services owner gives you printing services for a value of $5,000, she makes only about $1,600.

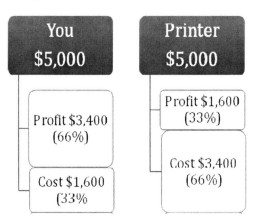

The print shop owner may get only around half of the profit on the same final price as do you, the restaurant owner. Remember, these numbers may vary so you need to look at your specific profit margin and situation, but a restaurant should be able to make more profit margin than a printing business.

For that reason, it is not the same for you to get $5,000 of advertisement placement as it is for a printer owner, because you have a higher profit margin. That's why you need to offer the printer owner a better deal.

Let's say you offer her $7,500 worth of advertising services for $5,000 worth of her printing services to you. Her cost will be 66% out of $5,000 = $3,400 but she is now getting $7,500 worth of advertising services.

This means that her cost saving is $7,500 - $3,400 = $4,100

You just helped her benefit more than an additional 50% from the deal ($1,600 + $4,100 = $5,700) instead of her regular 33% ($1,600) profit.

Now you are offering her to trade advertising time in exchange for the printed materials that you need, but at a rate of $1 to $1.75 in her favor.

You are offering her $7,500 worth of advertising for printing goods with a retail price of $5,000; you're offering the printing business owner something she can definitely use – at a better discount than she could ever get on her own.

I will illustrate the whole transaction with a graphic:

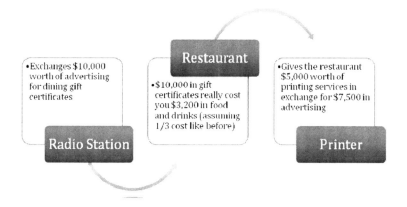

- Exchanges $10,000 worth of advertising for dining gift certificates

Radio Station

Restaurant

- $10,000 in gift certificates really cost you $3,200 in food and drinks (assuming 1/3 cost like before)

- Gives the restaurant $5,000 worth of printing services in exchange for $7,500 in advertising

Printer

Chances are, she'll accept your deal. Why shouldn't she?

You're giving her $7,500 worth of advertising credit – something she would have to normally pay real cash for. In return she'll give you $5,000 in printing services that probably cost her no more than $3,400 maximum.

The printing business, which normally makes less than 33% percent on new sales, increases its profit potential. She invests $3,400 to get $7,500.

And what about you? What's in it for you?

1. Well you traded $10,000 worth of restaurant gift certificates (which, we say at most, would cost you $3,400) for $10,000 worth of advertising coupons from the radio station.

2. You used $7,500 dollars in advertising coupons to pay for your printing services for a retail value of $5,000, saving $1,800 in cash. Remember, you still only invested the original $3,400 in gift certificates get them).

3. Your restaurant gift certificates (redeemable for only $25 each, as we mentioned before) will bring you many new customers that will try your restaurant for the first time, and hopefully will become frequent clients. This is an additional source of advertising for you.

4. Chances are good you won't have to honor the restaurant gift certificates for a long time because either the radio station or the people receiving them may not redeem them for a while. Until they come in and use them, you don't actually spend a dime.

5. Since your prices will likely rise over the next few years (adjusting for inflation or because your business is thriving and you can afford to raise prices, etc.), by the time the radio stations or their clients use all of the gift certificates, their purchasing power has diminished.

In essence, the radio or television stations or publications end up "financing" your $10,000 gift certificates for months or years – at no interest to you! The longer the station or publisher takes to redeem their gift certificates, the less it will cost you.

If this is beginning to sound incredible - wait: It gets better.

So, what happens with the rest of the barter value?

Remember that you originally traded for $10,000 in advertising, but you only used $7,500 with the printer on exchange for $5,000 in printing services? What happens to the remaining $2,500?

$10,000 in advertising dollars

Gave the Printer $7,500 in ad dollars	Got $5,000 in printing services	Still holding $2,500 in ad dollars

Let's summarize the deal so far:

1. You have invested $10,000 worth of radio advertising coupons for a food cost value of $3,400.

2. From these $10,000 advertising coupons, you gave $7,500 to the printing company in exchange for $5,000 worth of printing services that you needed.

3. In the previous transaction, you've already saved $1,800 in cash that you would have had to pay for the $5,000 out-of-pocket (remember, it cost you only $3,400 to get the advertising coupons that you've traded)

4. You still have left $2,500 worth of advertising coupons. This $2,500 value is extra "profit" for you. You may keep it for yourself to use if you need to promote your place or announce a

special event. You can also offer it to another retailer or service provider for a discounted price.

When you want to use your $2,500 credit, you can use the same model that you did with the printing business, offering another service provider the $2,500 at a discounted price so that these advertising coupons are attractive to them. Remember, these are pure profit for you, so anything you get for them is gravy.

So let's say that you need to get your restaurant freshly painted. You find a good painting company and they'll charge you $1,500 for the job. They are probably also making a 33% profit margin here so their cost is around $1,000 (I am rounding to simplify).

You could just pay cash, or you can use bartering, talk to the owners and offer them $2,500 in advertising in exchange for $1,500 in painting services (that cost them $1,000). They save $1,000 and you get another $1,500 on top of the $1,800 that you've already saved from the printing services.

This makes a total of $3,300 dollars in savings for you, and this is without taking into consideration the value of gift certificates that will get lost or forgotten, or that will be redeemed months or years later.

BARTERING DEAL YOUR SAVINGS

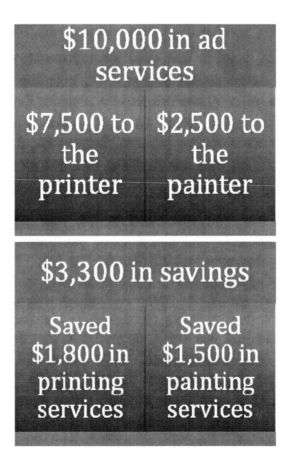

Please notice that you are selling the painters the advertising dollars at a discount, that's why you get less cash than the $2,500 that you have in advertising coupons. Also, remember that you could also use the advertising yourself if you have some kind of event that you want to promote.

So for an investment of $3,400 in food cost, you get $6,500 worth of services ($5,000 in printing services and $1,500 in painting services) that you needed without having to advance any money up front.

I would say that this is a pretty good deal, don't you think?

But you are not the only who benefits from this deal:

- The print shop owner gets $7,500 worth of advertising for a cost of $3,400 (saving $4,100 dollars)

- The painting crew owner also gets a good deal since they get $2,500 worth of advertising money and for a cost of around $1,000 (saving $1,500)

- The radio station benefits by selling advertising slots they have available at a premium price of $10,000 in restaurant gift certificates that they can give to their employees, use for radio promotions, give away to their listeners, etc.

Triangular Bartering should be a win/win/win proposition for all parties involved!

I use the printing and painting examples only as an illustration. In truth, almost any conceivable combination of goods or services, or any other variable can be used in triangulation to achieve your objective.

Other Bartering Possibilities

Another possibility is to make a deal with your local Chamber of Commerce, City Hall or any municipal organization that distributes a newsletter or other communication vehicle (direct mailing to the residents, web site, etc.) that they may have. You just need to approach the organization and offer it gift certificates to your restaurant in exchange for advertising in their newsletter or mailing.

In this way, it not only looks like your place gets endorsed by a respected organization but, most likely, your clients will see the chairperson and/or Council members or other well-known and respected members of the community dining at your place. You get a double benefit: exposure (by way of advertising) and distinguished clients that will attract other clients and give prestige to your establishment.

I hope that you see the point. Bartering is a great way to leverage, to optimize your resources in a creative way without costing you additional revenue. It is a multiplier of your assets.

And, by the way, you can also use a mixed model. Without trying to be confusing, you could offer the printing company $2,000 in direct gift certificates from your restaurant and $3,000 in advertising from the radio station.

Just be creative. You can adapt this model to fit everyone's needs.

Always identify the real needs of the person who controls the goods or services you want, and then satisfy those needs. You will get results.

The great thing about bartering is that you'll never lose money, because you are investing gift certificates for a dining experience in your place that cost you less than the actual value.

Remember:

- The cost of your food and drinks is spread over a longer period as people use the gift certificates .

- The gift certificates are also an advertising tool by themselves since they will bring you new customers that will discover your restaurant and become clients.

You can also use bartering to diversify and increase your sales. For example, you could start selling some high quality preserves or cheeses or some other precooked goods that match your restaurant's specialty.

If you have an Italian restaurant, you can sell Italian cheeses, balsamic vinegar, extra virgin olive oil, salamis, pre-packed prosciutto, etc. We will talk in more detail about how to increase the sales per customer in Chapter 9.

With bartering in mind, you can get these goods from the providers in exchange for gift certificates, or in a mixed model of some cash and some gift certificates.

You can also use the power of leverage and get these goods free of charge by splitting the profits with the provider after you sell the goods. In this way, you don't have to pay anything in advance. Your up-front cost is zero and you only have a profit.

As you can see, with a little creativity from your side, the possibilities are endless.

H O M E W O R K

This is the homework for this chapter:

1. Have a conversation with your accountant or pull the numbers from your computer to know what profit margin you get from each of your current dishes. Then you can get an average. (This profit margin percentage number will help you negotiate the terms of the bartering.)

2. Think about and write down a list of goods or services that you need - and are paying for - at the present. It may be a good idea to go over your books (or to ask your accountant if you have one) and find out what expenses you had the previous year on these services.

    This will be a good start for your list.

3. Think about (and write down) a list of goods or services that you desire (even if you are not using them now because of cash-flow problems).

4. Pick the top three businesses or service providers from points 2 and 3.

5. For each of these three businesses or service providers, think how much money you would be willing to trade in gift certificates. (Again, make them small; around $25 is a great target, lower if you are a fast food place).

6. Think about other businesses whose goods or services you don't need, but you think will accept gift certificates from your restaurant, and can be used for the triangulation bartering deals.

7. Contact the businesses that you want to trade with and offer them the gift certificates to your place in exchange for their services. You can use a mixed model if they don't want or need to trade for so much discounted dining value.

By the way, if you feel uneasy about going around and negotiating gift certificates, perhaps one of your employees would be better for the task. Do you remember our previous conversation about Strengths in Chapter 4?

- Pick a member of your staff who has good sales skills (probably one of your waiters will fit the bill since they are selling to your clients every day) and explain to them the bartering program.

- Offer them a compensation (performance based would be the best) for their work.

Happy Bartering!

In the next chapter we will talk about Geometric Growth. This is the growth that you want to achieve in order to leave behind most of your competitors.

Chapter 7:
Geometric Growth

Stop thinking linearly

Most business owners try to grow their business in order to grow their income. However, they usually try to grow their business linearly, focusing on one area of growth at a time. Not many restaurant owners set up a goal for themselves by thinking linearly.

So you spent some time creating a strategy. Perhaps looking at the results from the previous year, you make a commitment to yourself to grow your business by 10% by the end of the year. You could increase your business in several ways:

- Bringing new clients in.

- Raising your menu prices so that your profit margin goes up.

- Changing your menu items, introducing new and more profitable dishes.

- Improving your employees' efficiency so that your clients are happier.

- Etc.

Focusing in one of these areas at a time is not effective.

You need to grow all the areas of your business simultaneously to really make an impact.

You need to grow your business **geometrically**, not **linearly**.

The Only 3 Ways to Grow Your Business

I know that you may be panicking, thinking "Oh my gosh, how many things do I need to focus on if I want to increase my business? I have enough to consider trying to increase the number of people who frequent my restaurant."

Don't panic. The good news is that there are basically three ways to grow a business. Here they are, nicely described for you:

1. Increase the number of clients who come to your restaurant.

2. Increase the amount of money that they spend per visit.

3. Increase the frequency of their visits (number of times that they dine at your place).

That's it - it doesn't look too difficult, does it?

So what can you do to grow your business geometrically instead of linearly?

It is very simple: you need to grow all three areas at the same time. Every small increment in each of these three areas will combine to create a geometrical growth.

Albert Einstein said once:

> *"The most powerful force in the universe is compound interest"*

Compound Interest uses the same idea as geometric growth (we could also call it compound growth).

I will illustrate this for you with an easy-to-follow example:

Let's assume (or substitute real numbers here) that you have 2,000 active clients a year in your restaurant. Each client spends an average of $40 dining, and they visit an average of three times a year as the chart below shows:

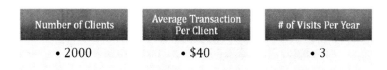

Number of Clients	Average Transaction Per Client	# of Visits Per Year
• 2000	• $40	• 3

This gives us a total yearly income of $240,000 (2,000 x $40 x 3)

Now, if we were following a linear strategy, we would focus on increasing the number of clients to make the additional 10% growth as follows:

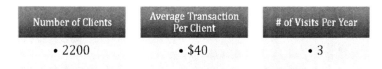

Number of Clients	Average Transaction Per Client	# of Visits Per Year
• 2200	• $40	• 3

This would give us a total income of $264,000, (2,200 x 40 x 3) which is exactly a 10% growth. Not too bad.

But what would happen if we grow all three categories by 10% simultaneously instead of only increasing the number of clients? Let's see:

Number of Clients	Average Transaction Per Client	# of Visits Per Year
• 2200	• $44	• 3.3

So we now have 2,200 clients x $44 per meal (a 10% increase in average ticket) x 3.3 visits (I know that you can't have 1/3 of a client, but we are using *average* number of visits).

This gives us a total of: $319,440 or a growth of 33.1%!

Now, we are talking!

And the example is only assuming a conservative 10% increase for each category. With all the tools that I will show you in the next three chapters, you will *be able to increase each of the categories more than 10% easily*!

Let's illustrate this with a graphic that compares Linear Growth (1 category at the time) versus Exponential Growth (all the 3 categories simultaneously). In this way, you can see how a modest increase in each of the categories combines to make a big total increase:

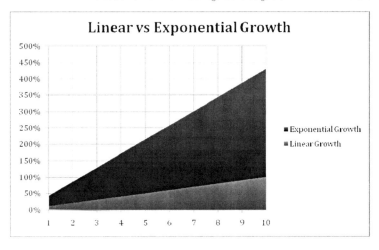

Exponential vs. Linear Growth and Why You Want to Grow Exponentially

You can see in this chart that if you were to grow your business linearly 10% a year, you would need 10 years to double your business. However, **if you increase 10% in each of the three categories, year after year, it would take you only THREE years to double your business!**

The funny part is that it costs the same amount of work and money to grow your business exponentially than it costs you to grow it linearly.

Don't you think that this is the way that you should operate?

You need to stop thinking linearly and think geometrically. This is the way to really grow a business and to make you leap way ahead of your competitors.

When you apply this multiple growth on the three ways to grow your business **simultaneously**, you will become a dominant force in your area/specialty.

It is like the military hitting the enemy with the full force of different approaches (sea attack, air attack, artillery, missiles, stealth, etc.) all at the same time. Nobody will be able to compete with you!

Areas of Improvement:

There is another aspect to look at in order to multiply your effectiveness and grow your restaurant business. Every business (yes, your place as well) has hidden assets, undiscovered opportunities, underperforming operations, underutilized resources and employees.

You need to periodically re-evaluate your operations, and examine with a magnifying glass each aspect of your business: raise the performance of each employee, each provider, and each process that you have.

There are approaches you can use in all aspects of your business that have the capacity to produce far greater returns on your money, effort and time you or your employees invest.

To maximize leverage, look for ways you can produce to get a greater result from every action, every task, every investment (financial or human) that you make; it is very doable.

Although this task may seem daunting, you can tackle it as you should tackle all big tasks: one step at a time.

Let's get down to it.

1. Write down the main processes that constitute your daily work. You may want to list by broad categories such as:

   - Food and Beverage Distributors

   - Front of the House Staff

   - Kitchen Staff

   - Clients (booking, sitting, service, etc.)

   - Operations

   - Marketing and Sales

   - Pricing

   - Finances

2. Review each process and break it down in tasks that are more manageable.

Let's review in more detail each of the above categories:

FOOD AND BEVERAGE DISTRIBUTORS

Are you getting the best value/quality possible for each category?

- Produce

- Meats

- Seafood

- Desserts,

- Wines/Beer

- Etc.

Analyze the distributors that you have for each category:

- Are they providing you with the best possible quality, service, timeliness and value?

- Are they flexible enough to accommodate a last-minute request for an emergency?

http://www.myrestaurantmarketing.com

- Do you know the owner of the company, or at least some high-ranking manager? (This could be important in negotiating a Joint Venture or additional revenue resources, as we will see in Chapter 8).

Perhaps, if the distributor is a large company, you should think about a smaller and hungrier one. You may be able to leverage the opportunity for your business, and negotiate better with a smaller and nimbler provider than with a very large one where the policies and bureaucracy are also large.

FRONT OF THE HOUSE STAFF

Remember what we said in Chapter 1 about evaluating your employees?

Do you have the most loyal, motivated, honest and best employees that you can afford? If not, please review Chapter 1 and do your homework.

Your front of the house staff, especially servers and hosts are your sales people - your marketing people - they represent your business to the clients. If they are not excellent, your restaurant can't be excellent.

Your restaurant standard will be set by your weakest link: food, service or process (delays, double-bookings, mistakes, etc.). Whatever your weakest link is, it defines the level of quality and excellence of your place.

Now (assuming that you are happy with your staff) if they are capable, smart and eager, or at least willing to make your business as successful as it can be, you need to work with them to improve your processes.

Trust me, no matter how much you know about your place and how many hours you spend at your premises (and you may be there all the time), your servers will notice things that you are not aware of that could be improved.

There is always room for improvement.

Don't be afraid; pick their brains and let them tell you things that you can do better, faster, cheaper. Get their feedback, analyze it, implement what is doable if it is worth it, reject it if it is not - but always thank them for their ideas. Promote an open communication where they feel that they mean something to you.

KITCHEN STAFF

Same thing with your kitchen labor: listen to them.

- Are they suggesting for you to change something to make the process of ordering and handling the food more efficient?

- Do they complain that the produce from your distributors comes damaged? That your fish is smelly?

Listen to what they have to say. Set up a formal weekly meeting with them where you hear their complaints, ideas, suggestions...

You will make them feel good, and I'm sure that you can learn one or two things from them.

CLIENTS

This is your most important asset. After all, they are the ones bringing you the money, paying for your bills, your employees, your expenses, and your lifestyle. If there are no clients, there is no business.

Think about your contact with your clients, starting way before they step into your restaurant.

You probably start engaging them in your marketing materials: your web site, your direct mailing, your newsletter, your coupons and ads are the first experience that these future clients have with your place.

Are you being honest and professional in all your communications?

I hope so. People are really good at detecting dishonesty, and they will stop doing business with you very quickly if they feel that you over-promise and under-deliver in your ads.

How about when they call to make reservations? Are they being treated the best possible way with respect, courtesy, affability and efficiency?

When they step into your door, is somebody waiting for them to greet them?

Are your employees genuinely interested in your clients' well being? In making sure that they enjoy the best possible experience available right from the beginning?

People are in their worst (patience, behavior) when they are hungry or thirsty. Make sure that they get seated promptly if they made reservations. Show them that you are concerned that they have to wait. Give them a free glass of wine or a little something to munch on while they are waiting. This will show them that you really care about them.

If - for whatever reason - they need to wait for a long time (hey, sometimes these things happen; I know by experience), make sure to offer them something complimentary when they finally are seated. Tell your servers to be especially attentive to their needs and try not to make them wait extra time for their food.

Do you have a good system to give your best clients the best seats? Regulars appreciate that you take notice and give them the best tables. Casual diners will understand getting just a fair table more easily than people who frequent your place. Your best clients need to be taken care of appropriately.

Try to remember their names, their stories. Your clients like to feel special, and their egos appreciate (especially if they bring guests) that you, as the owner of the place, recognize them as your best clients and ask them about their health, their loved ones, etc.

OPERATIONS

Do you have a mechanism that points out when something is wrong? Do you have an established written process to deal with problems that all your employees are familiar with? If not, you should.

For example, what's your policy if a dish arrives cold or if the client doesn't like it? Do you tell your people to exchange it with a new one and apologize to the client with a smile?

What about if somebody waits for their reservation for half an hour? Do you give them a free appetizer? Free entree? Even a complimentary meal if the diner is one of your best clients?

If not, you should think about scenarios like these.

Acknowledging and correcting poor performance will make them forgive the bad moments. Also they will tell all their friends about how well your establishment deals with problems. Yes, you lose one meal (and really only the cost of the meal), but you win a client for life, and trust me, they will pay you back a hundred times the cost of that meal - instead of never returning again.

MARKETING AND SALES

What's your Marketing Strategy? Do you have one?

What about your Marketing message? At this point of the book, you should have a Unique Selling Proposition (USP) and a clear vision of where you want to go and what you want to accomplish.

Do your marketing materials (all of them) reflect this USP? This vision?

Evaluate all your communications and all your advertising, and make sure that all your employees know and live your vision and USP.

Also, are you using the most efficient and effective marketing that you can?

Do you spend a lot of money in the Yellow Pages or other forms of advertising, but you can't quantify the results?

This is a common mistake. I know many restaurant owners that spend thousands of dollars in promoting their business in the Yellow Pages by displaying half page or even a whole page advertisement.

Now think about this, how many new clients will go to your restaurant because they see the ad in the Yellow Pages? Probably not many.

I don't know anybody who wants to dine out and say to himself or herself: *"Hmm, I feel like French food but I don't know any good French restaurant. Let me go to the Yellow Pages and look for the French Restaurant with the biggest ad. This must mean that they are good"*.

Perhaps some older people or people traveling for business would do this, but I can guarantee you that you won't recoup the money that you invest in the big ad. It is different for other professions like a plumber or carpet cleaner. You look in the Yellow Pages when you need a service like this, but it doesn't work for restaurants.

Same thing with newspapers or magazines: You can spend a fortune advertising in them; but you almost certainly won't recoup your money.

If you don't believe me, do the math. It is easy:

Let's assume that your average price per client is $40, and from this you get $20 in profit. So for every customer that the Yellow Pages or newspaper ad brings in, you get $20. This is just an approximation; use your own actual numbers with to determine average prices and profits to be accurate.

Now, if you pay $2,000 for your ad, this means that you need to get 100 new clients just to break even. Every client on top of the 100 will be profit.

Do you really think that a Yellow Pages ad will bring you 100 clients?

I don't think so. And be aware that your restaurant will still be listed in the Yellow Pages even if you don't pay a dime. The only difference is the size of the listing. By default you will be listed in the appropriate category but you won't have any big ad to display.

And who cares? People searching for restaurants in the Yellow Pages are most likely not the people looking for a good place to go. They are probably looking for the phone number of a specific restaurant to make a reservation anyway.

So where *do* people look for restaurants?

That's easy! They ask their friends, their relatives, their coworkers or they go to the Web to places like www.CitySearch.com, www.restaurants.com, www.yelp.com, www.zagat.com, etc., look for the category of restaurant of their liking, and read the reviews from other people who went there.

This is where deeply caring for and loving your clients pays tremendous benefits.

If your clients are very happy with your food, with your service and your attention to them, they will recommend you to all the people who they know. And they will write excellent reviews in the online sites about your place...

In other words, they will be your advocates, your sales force and will bring many new clients who want to experience the same level of excellence that you give all your clients.

PRICING

Do you know your food cost per dish? Your profit margin per drink?

Sometimes the most expensive dishes are not the ones that give you the most profit, and that is true for wines or the rest of the alcoholic drinks.

What I am trying to say is that you need to be smart and create menu dishes that don't cost you and your clients a fortune and leave you with a very small profit margin.

You (or your chef following your instructions) can create wonderful dishes with great quality - but not too exotic or expensive - that your clients will love, and will still leave you a substantial profit margin.

Do the same with the wines or mixed drinks.

Select wines with great value and also excellent quality, and pass your savings to your clients. If you look hard enough, you will find excellent wines that you can buy at a good price from your distributors.

Work with them. Remember that we also care about them, they are our friends and allies and we need to establish great relationships and expect great service from them. Tell them that you are looking for quality and great value - even if they are less well known.

WINE LIST

Create a nice looking wine list where you explain to your clients about the wines: their special features, taste, the best food pairing with menu items, etc.

Many times people don't order wine because they feel intimidated by their lack of knowledge, and they think that they will look stupid if they ask the basic questions.

Here is a great idea for you to increase your wine sales at the same time that you help your clients:

Create a special wine list - or even better - a good looking wine book with a photo of the wine label, description of the wine, map with its region, etc., and assign a unique number to each wine. Use a number or a combination of a letter and a number, using the letter as the initial for the class of wine. For example, you could have Red (R), White (W), Champagne (C), Dessert Wine (D) or Port (P) followed by the number.

On your food menu, label each item with the wine code corresponding to the wines that go well with the menu item. This way many clients will know which wine goes together with the food, or at the least they may be curious and ask to see your wine list to learn more about the wine. And this could lead to extra wine sales.

Also, some clients will feel more comfortable ordering the wine by its number instead of trying to pronounce the wine name, especially international wines and domestic wines that have French, Spanish or Italian names.

If you want to get ever more client-friendly in your wine list, you could use color-coded labels to indicate price ranges. For example, green labels could mean wines in the $15 to $25 price range, yellow labels between $26 to $45, orange $46 to $85, and red $86 and over. This is just an example - you can come up with your own system.

There is an Internet marketing expert that always says: "A confused mind always says NO". The easier that you make it for your clients to select wine, the more wine that you'll sell. Always remember that your ultimate goal is to lower the barrier and make easy for your clients to choose a wine.

FINANCES

I would recommend to you: get yourself a good point-of-sale system. Not only will it allow you to improve the food ordering process, keep track of your inventory, and create accurate financial statements for your accountant, but it will also give you invaluable information to keep track of your best and worst sellers, etc.

Once a year, print a list of your dishes organized by sales, from best sellers to worst. Perhaps you can do this on January 2nd so that you start the year with a clean slate. You can choose any date you wish. Just be consistent.

Scrap the last 3 to 5 dishes (depending how large your menu is) starting from the bottom and moving up the list, and replace them with new dishes that hopefully will produce much better sales.

This elimination process is not guesswork; it is based on actual choices made by the clients, **your** clients. After all, they are the ones who order the food and tell you with their wallets what works and what doesn't.

By eliminating the worst sellers, you keep your menu fresh and updated, and satisfy the majority of your clients.

Make sure that you repeat this exercise at least once or twice a year if you have the energy and/or time. I wouldn't recommend doing it more than once every 6 months since you may not have enough information to be statistically meaningful - plus it is a lot of work.

If you keep track of your food cost on the computer, you can easily sort information and print reports that tell you which menus give you the most profit: final price minus combined cost of the ingredients. This may require extra work, and many restaurant owners never take the time to enter the information, but I strongly recommend that you add this step since you'll harvest the benefits later on.

This is very valuable information since you can play with your menus to maximize your profit per dish in several ways (remember that we touched on this point at the beginning of this Financial section).

You need to accomplish one or more of the following tasks:

- Eliminate the menu dishes that give you the least amount of profit (less than 20% for example).

- Raise the price of some dishes if necessary so that you keep your profit margin.

- Replace some of the most expensive ingredients for others that are cheaper but still give you similar results. This works better for standard menu items than it does for gourmet, exclusive, higher-priced restaurants.

Attention: I am not suggesting here that you replace good quality ingredients for cheap imitations. I am suggesting to replace, for example, Dungeness crab (very expensive) for less expensive crab or crabmeat, if this doesn't make a big difference in the taste of the dish. And, of course you shouldn't continue to call it "Dungeness Crab Extravaganza" or similar, since this would be misleading your clients.

In whatever you do in your life: it costs you the same effort, the same amount of time and equal energy to do something and produce result X as it does to do something else and produce two, four and even eight times better results. And this doesn't only apply to your restaurant, but also to your relationships, your hobbies, your friends and family, etc.

The effort is the same; the difference is the strategy.

There are aspects of your business and your life that you can increase, improve and multiply exponentially by changing the <u>way</u> you do things.

You should aim to get a greater outcome from every action, every effort, every investment (in money and time) that you make, and this is not only possible but also totally doable.

But remember what we said in Chapter 1:

You can't get a lot until you give a lot. It is a simple rule but very powerful.

We don't have a homework section in this chapter, since the homework has been included as part of the text.

In the next chapter, Chapter 8, we will cover the first way to grow a business: Increasing the number of clients who come to your restaurant. I will tell you the best ways to attract new people to your place.

Chapter 8: Increasing the Number of Clients

What's the Best Way to Attract More People to Your Place?

I n this chapter we will focus on the first of the three

ways to grow your business. Do you remember them? I will spell them out for you once more:

1. Increase the number of clients who come to your restaurant.

2. Increase the amount of money that they spend per visit.

3. Increase the frequency of their visits (number of times per month/year that they dine at your place).

Increasing the number of clients involves not only bringing new clients to your place, it also means bringing back former clients that haven't visited your place in a while for whatever reason (perhaps they weren't happy with your former way of doing business or they just forgot about your place. Hey - it happens!).

Increasing the number of customers is the initiative where restaurant owners focus and spend most of their money when they think about growing their business. That's also the area where most of the restaurant advertising sales people put their emphasis on, and this explains why restaurants spend a lot of money in bringing new people through their doors.

However, trying to get new clients (also called prospecting) is the least effective of all of your marketing initiatives.

This doesn't seem logical; after all, most of the restaurateurs expend the bulk of their marketing budgets to bring new prospect instead of focusing on the clients that they already have or have had.

This is a very important aspect of growing your business. But after you finish this book and start implementing all the strategies, recommendations, ideas and tips that we are covering here, you'll realize that you don't need to put as much emphasis on getting *new* clients in order to grow your business as you should in the other two strategies (covered in the next two chapters).

Before we move forward, let's clarify some definitions that I will be using so that you don't get confused:

Prospect: A prospect is a potential customer. It's a person that you mail, email, advertise to, etc. hoping that they will walk through your door.

Customer: A customer is a prospect that has reacted positively to your marketing campaign and decided to try your place. He/She is somebody who will come and eat at least once at your restaurant. A customer is a step up from a prospect.

Client: A client is a recurrent customer. It is a person who tried your place, liked it and decided to come several times. This person is your goal and the one who'll bring you most of your income. You need to focus all your energy in converting customers into clients.

Also, before we talk in detail about how to bring new clients to your restaurant, you need to understand a very important concept that will have profound implications in the way that you spend your marketing dollars.

This concept will help you understand why you should focus your marketing mainly in the other two categories.

It is called the Lifetime Value of a client.

Lifetime Value of a Client

How much would your business improve if you could bring in an extra 10 clients this month? What about an extra 100?

Wouldn't you be willing to invest in these customers if you know that they'll become your clients, even if you don't make a huge profit on the first transaction? Shouldn't you instead nurture <u>these</u> people so that they will come over and over to your place?

These are very important questions that have essential consequences in the way that you'll spend your marketing money.

So let's try to understand what a client is worth to you in profit over their buying lifetime at your establishment. Remember, you must first have a great place with excellent service so they will come over and over - that's the plan.

We need to calculate the profit that every client can generate for you minus all the expenses that you have for advertising, marketing and service to them.

This exercise is aimed to understand the individual's **"Lifetime Value of a Client"**. It is the estimated profit that a recurrent client will bring to your place over a period of 5 years. We assume 5 years per client since this is the average time that American people live in one place.

You will be very surprised to learn how much money your clients are worth to your business.

We will use an example to demonstrate this point:

Let's assume that the average new customer that comes through the door brings an average profit of $20 in the first sale, and, after having a great dining experience, becomes a client by coming back once a month for a total of 12 times a year. This is a realistic goal if you really cultivate your clients and make your place the best restaurant that it can be.

So, let's see: $20 x 12 = $240.

If this client frequents your restaurant during 5 years, before they move out of the area or just stop going to your place, he/she will be worth it to you $1,200 in pure profit ($240 x 5 = $1,200). Of course, you need to adjust this formula to fit your particular profit, but this will help you understand the concept.

Now, most your clients won't come alone, they will come with at least one other person: their significant others, friends and family, etc. Let's be conservative and double the profit number to $2,400 (assuming that they will come with one more person).

This $2,400 per client is your **Restaurant Marginal Net Worth (RMNW)** and it is a very important number as we will see in the rest of this chapter.

Now, you know how much (on average) you can get from every regular client, and can use that number to determine how much to spend in capturing your customers and turning them into clients.

Do you see now why it's very important that you really take care of your clients? What's a free meal (if you need to compensate for a mistake or a bad experience) to make a customer a happy returning client? You would spend $15 or $20 on a client that will give you $2,400 back!

If this isn't the greatest investment that you can make, I don't know what is!

Once you know precisely how to quantify the marginal net worth of a client, then you can work with the data. Even if it costs you $40 or $50 to get a new customer and convert him or her into a client or to bring back your existing and inactive clients, this is still a great investment.

You need to know how much you can get out of repeat clients before you can make a conscious decision about how much to spend in your marketing.

Imagine a funnel where at the top you "pour in" for prospects (with some targeted marketing) that you can convert into customers who ultimately will become clients, repeatedly coming to your place for many years.

I will illustrate the process with a graphic, so that you can better get the concept:

Lifetime Value

Ultimately I want you to spend less money acquiring each client, but for now we need to get your restaurant full of happy people before we can change your focus into getting more out of them - and increasing their visit frequency (the second and third ways to grow your business).

Take a reading break now, go to the Homework page and follow the steps to calculate your clients' Lifetime Value.

Attracting New Clients

Now that you understand the Lifetime Value of a client, let's talk about what can you do to attract more people to your place.

What can you do to convert these people into clients? Into high quality repeated clients? Into the kind of clients that *you* want?

We mentioned before some things that don't work: Yellow Pages, newspaper ads (unless you use them to communicate a special event or occasion), radio ads and TV advertising (they are too expensive and very seldom bring enough new people to justify their investment).

So what does work? The key for you to understand is: you need to do marketing that gives you measurable results.

You need to be able to know how many new people walk through the doors of your restaurant, and how many clients come back to your place because of your marketing

What marketing vehicles do we have available that can give us these numbers?

There are several that we can use. We'll cover some of them in this chapter. Later (in Chapter 10) we will cover more specific marketing tactics to increase the frequency of visits from your current clients.

Let's examine in detail the following marketing strategies to attract new customers: Coupons, Targeted Direct Mailing, Join Ventures and Networking.

At the end, please keep your clients' satisfaction and dinning experience in mind at all times. Don't try to put so many up-selling systems that you alienate your clients and make them angry about your sales pressure.

Start slowly. Implement one or two of these ideas at the time and always, always, ask for feedback to your clients. They will tell you what they like and what they don't.

You will be surprised how many of these ideas will be very welcome by your clientele and not only they will increase your profit and sales per client, but also will make your restaurant unique and different from your competitors.

Coupons

Coupons are great marketing investments if you target the right audience. There are franchise companies such as R.S.V.P (you can check them at http://www.rsvppublications.com/) that mail classy postcards to a medium to high-income market, based on the value of their houses.

Postcards are great because people read them right away. It's less work than having to open an envelope before even knowing what's inside. Many envelopes end in the recycling bin (or worse, in the trash can) before they are ever opened.

The great thing about coupons is that people must bring them to your place to redeem them. This allows you to collect these coupons. Please tell your servers to deposit the coupons in a special box you can keep in the kitchen or at a server station. Always count how many coupons you've received and determine your extra revenue and profit.

Think carefully about what kind of offers you want to put on your coupons.

Please remember that the goal for now is to attract new prospects that will hopefully become clients. Once you have established your Unique Selling Proposition or USP, put your clients at the top of your priorities and create a money-back guarantee (as we saw before) so you can show them you want their business.

Eventually, you won't need to use coupons anymore - once your place is full and we implement other mechanisms to keep your clients spending more money with you and coming back over and over again.

And, remember when we talked about bartering? Try to make a deal with the coupon company owner; offer to trade some (or all) of the upfront price in exchange for gift certificates. Again, try to arrange no higher value than $20 or $25 for each, since this will bring you more customers.

If you still like to try ads in newspapers and magazines, please include a coupon in the ad that must be redeemed, so that you can track how many people show because of the ad. You can offer a free entrée, a discount or some other enticement so that they feel motivated to bring the coupon to your restaurant. Every month, count the coupons, check the numbers and see if the expense was worth it to you.

Remember, you always need to be able to measure your marketing initiatives. Otherwise you may be spending unnecessary money in ineffective marketing.

PROS AND CONS OF A COUPON CAMPAIGN:

Although coupons are great marketing investments if used correctly, as with everything in life they have their pros and cons. Let's briefly examine both sides:

P R O S :

- **It is hands off marketing.** You contact a coupon company, pay them and they take care of everything so it doesn't use your time, just your money.

- **It is measurable:** You can measure the results by collecting the coupons and tracking the number of guests they bring to your place (and include others that come with them).

C O N S :

- **You can't control the target audience.** Although this could be mitigated if you select a coupon company that targets a broad segment of your average clientele.

- **It could be expensive.** At least as expensive as other marketing initiatives, but again this could be alleviated with a good bartering deal with the coupon company.

- **You can't control when the coupon mailing happens.** Coupon companies usually do their mailing quarterly so you can't decide when to send the coupons to maximize your weaker months.

To conclude with this section: although usually the good coupon strategies could be very valuable for your business, there are other ways (cheaper ways) to attract high quality, high-income prospects to your place by using Targeted Mailings.

Targeted Mailing

We agreed that postcards are better than sales letters, right? If you are not convinced yet, think about yourself, you will never toss a postcard before reading it, but I'm sure that you throw away many un-open solicitation letters. On top of that, it is cheaper to mail a postcard than to mail a letter. It is a win-win situation.

So then we just need to buy postcards. I recommend you to create them online at a print place such as <u>Vista Print</u> or barter gift certificates on exchange for postcards at a local printer house. I also recommend you to mail them yourself instead of paying thousands of dollars to coupon companies.

The only problem is to find the high-income, targeted audience, who will be likely to frequent your place and spend the money. If only we knew whom these people were!

Well, the good news is that we know who they are and I will tell you exactly where and how to get them!

Who has high income, great reputation, many connections, extensive networking and it's easily available and public?

The answer is: Local Professionals.

Think about it! They want you to find them. They are easily discoverable so that you don't need to search for them. You can easily find them in both:

- **Old fashion way:** Yellow Pages Book

- **More high tech way:** Online Yellow Pages or other online professional directories easily available via any search engine.

Now, you need to think about what kind of Professionals you would like to attract to your place. Do you want Lawyers?, Doctors?, Accountants?, Builders?, Perhaps Architects?...

Do you want to specialize in one category and target your marketing to them?

BUILDING A LIST WITH YOUR PROSPECTS

Whichever segment you decide, the first step is to build a list with the names and addresses of the people who you want to target to.

This is not as complicated as it sounds. If you are a bit computer savvy, you can do this yourself or have somebody from your staff doing it for you. Remember the chapter about delegating tasks that you are not excellent at?

There are two ways to create and maintain your list if you decide to do it in house:

1. If you use Microsoft Windows, you can create a database in your computer with a program like Microsoft Excel or better yet Microsoft Access or any other database program.

2. If you use Mac computers, you can also use Excel, but I would recommend you to use Bento. Bento is an inexpensive and very easy to use, yet powerful, database for Mac (you can check it here: http://www.filemaker.com/products/bento/overv iew.html). If you are a sophisticated database user, you can also use the more powerful (and more expensive) FileMaker (http://www.filemaker.com/).

The advantage of getting your list online is that you can copy the information from the web and paste it into an Excel sheet or database and then do mail merge to create the labels or print directly onto the postcards. There is also the option to outsource this whole list management and postcard creation process to outside companies. You can buy lists of audiences targeted to your core clientele. Some companies that

sell   targeted   lists   are   Nextmark
(http://www.nextmark.com/   )   or   Totally   Traffic:
(http://www.totally-traffic.com/). You can search in
Google for more if you like more choices.

You can also outsource the printing and distribution of
the postcards. For example Vista Print has an option
where you provide them with an initial list (database)
and they will upload it to their database and print the
names directly in the postcards. This is a great
alternative if you don't want to do the work yourself.
You can check more details at Vista Print

So now that you have your list, what can you put in
your postcards to make them attractive?

Well, you could write in your postcard: *"Come to the
Black Olive, and meet some of your peers while you
eat. We give special discounts to lawyers so you will
meet many other colleagues here."* Or something like
this; you get the point.

Or perhaps you just want to give them a good offer in
your postcard so that they will come and check your
place.

You want to really call their attention and bring them
to your place since not only they make excellent
prospects, but also they could use your restaurant as
their place to meet and entertain their customers and
colleagues.

Give them an attractive offer such as a coupon valid for one free meal.

You really want and need to bring these high quality people!

PROS AND CONS OF A TARGETED MAILING:

We decided that Target Mailing is a great marketing investment, but again it has some pros and cons. I will spell them out for you.

P R O S :

- **You can totally target your audience.** If you decide to pursue direct mailing, you can create (or buy) lists of audiences targeted to your core clientele.

- **You control the timing.** Since you have total control, you can decide when you mail the coupons to fill in your place whenever the business is slower.

- **It's cheaper.** You don't need to pay a coupon company, just the cost of the postcards. You will pay only once a photographer and/or graphic artist to create the postcard and then you can reprint them over and over.

- **It is measurable:** Again, you can measure the results by collecting the coupons and counting how many people did they bring to your place

C O N S :

- **It can take lots of your time.** You need to create the lists or have somebody creating the lists for you. This is not difficult if you want to target to local professionals, for example, since they are all in the yellow pages.

- **Creating the lists sometimes could be difficult**. If you target a broader audience such as families, if you own a family restaurant, is not as simple since you can't use the yellow pages.

- **You need to be computer savvy**. Or have somebody from your staff doing this task since the lists will live in a database and you'll be using your computer to create mailing labels.

- **You need to be organized and on top of it.** Or you will procrastinate and forget to send the postcards, etc.

Let's look now at other ways to bring more prospects to your place. The next one could bring you lots of high quality people if done correctly. It is worth it to explore.

Join Ventures with Other Businesses

Question for you: Who has already clients that you want?

If you have a middle-to-upper scale restaurant, and you want high net worth clients, there are many other businesses that cater to the higher income audience. I am talking about business such as Luxury Car Dealers, Jewelries, High End Furniture Stores, Expensive Photographers, Yacht Dealers, etc.

If, on the other hand, you have a fast food or family restaurant, perhaps you can make deals with carpet cleaners, dry cleaning places, hair saloons or any other business whose core clients are similar to yours.

This is how it works:

1. Approach the owners of these businesses, or better yet, invite them over for a free lunch or dinner to your place, so that they can experience your restaurant by themselves. This will work best in person, since establishing a personal relationship with these people will open the doors of cooperation much quicker.

2. Offer them Gift Certificates at half price. They can buy from you each $25 gift certificate for $12.50

3. The business owners can give these gift certificates (one or more) to their best clients as a token of their appreciation. Their clients will be very happy to receive a $25 gift certificate and won't ever know that they business only paid half for this.

You don't make any profit for the people who will bring this gift certificate but you won't expend much money either since you only paid $12.50 for each so pretty much each new customer that you'll convert into clients will break even.

Do you remember the value of a client to you? It could mean $2,400 potential dollars in the future for $0 marketing cost so I think that this is a pretty good deal.

If the business owners refuse to pay you for the gift certificates, you could still offer them the gift certificates for free (in this case, for a smaller amount, like $15).

Remember, a $15 gift certificate means that you only lose the value of your food: around $8 or $9 dollars for each transaction, and you can assume that they will spend more money because of the low price of the gift certificates.

This is a very cheap price to bring new potential clients to your place!

You can do this with several businesses at the same time until you reach a point where you don't need to bring new prospects to your place anymore.

The next method that we will use is my favorite one: Implementing a Formalized Referral System.

How to Setup a Formalized Referral System

What are your main marketing vehicles now?

If you look at all your marketing investments and expenses, what percentage of all your business is produced as a result of your marketing?

How many new potential clients do you bring because of your investment in marketing?

When I asked this question to many restaurant owners, they concluded that most of their clients comes from referrals or walk-ins because they saw the restaurant. Only a small part of their traffic comes as a result of their investments in marketing. However 100% of their effort is spent running ads and promotions.

This doesn't make any logical sense. Why wouldn't you want to redirect your efforts to create a formalized referral system that can bring you ten times more people, ten times more quality people than any ad that you may spend your money on?

Referrals are perhaps the most powerful weapon that you have in your Marketing arsenal.

TOP 5 BENEFITS FROM USING REFERRALS

These are some of the top 5 benefits that you get from using Referrals as a Marketing Strategy:

1. It is very inexpensive to implement.

2. It brings quality people who you'll be able to convert into clients.

3. It gives you instantaneous credibility. People trust their friends and colleagues much more than any brochure, flyer or ad that you can create.

4. It fills your restaurant with people who are connected. They will be visiting your business more often with the hope that they will meet their friends, colleagues, acquaintances, etc.

http://www.myrestaurantmarketing.com

5. It keeps people talking about your place and therefore fresh in their minds.

Now, if your place is good, you probably already have some kind of informal referral system where happy clients recommend your restaurant to their family and friends but what we need is to create a formalized referral system.

Look at how many referrals you get without doing anything right now. You could potentially double your business by setting up a formalized referral system.

Statistics show that a referral-generated client normally spends more money, comes to your place more often and it's more profitable and loyal than other potential clients that you may have acquired by any other marketing vehicles.

Just by thinking about it, putting in place a process (system) and letting all your staff knows about it, you will greatly multiply the effect and efficacy of your marketing.

If correctly implemented, a formal referral system is perhaps the only marketing tool that you will ever need, and the best part is that it will cost you almost nothing in marketing materials (just the cost of the gift certificates).

The beauty of this system is that it has very little downside (just the cost of printing), and unlimited potential.

5 EASY STEPS TO SETUP A FOOLPROOF REFERRAL SYSTEM

I've just put together for you a foolproof system that you can use. Just follow these easy 5 steps and you'll be on your way to have a great Referral System:

1. **Create Special Referral Gift Certificates**

   Make them all for a maximum amount of $20 to $25 and make sure that they are marked as **Referral Gift Certificates.** Make them different from your regular gift certificates.

   Make a space in this Referral Gift Certificates for the name of your best clients and another space for the name of the recipients. Your Clients will give these certificates to the recipients of their choice.

   Also make sure to add a legend saying that they can't be added or combined with any other offers. The idea is that each gift certificate will bring at least one person. They will hopefully bring two or more if they don't come along to your place.

2. Identify your best clients.

Usually people mingle and socialize with other people similar in tastes, education, income level, etc. If you have great clients, who are happy to go to your place and to spend money in great food, they most likely know other people like them.

Meet with your Servers and explain the program to them. Together with your staff, brainstorm and make a list of your best clients. Please don't neglect to include your employees in this step. After all, they know (or should know if they are any good) who your best clients are.

You can of course, add to this list each time that a recognizable face enters your restaurant. Just make sure that your staff is always in the lookout for good clients!

3. Approach these clients at the end of their meal.

Ask them if their dining experience was excellent and everything was up to their liking. If they respond positive (or even better yet, if they respond enthusiastically), explain to them that you really appreciate their business and enjoy their company.

Since they probably associate with other people like themselves, who mirror their values and tastes, you would like to extend your great service and quality to those people as well, so that they can try your restaurant.

Tell them that you are trying to promote, for people who are regular clients, to bring their friends and relatives since you want to have your restaurant full of people just like them, who appreciate good food and service.

They should like this talk; after all, we all like to be recognized and praised!

4. **Give them 4 Gift Certificates (1 for them and 3 to give away to their friends and family).**

At this point, I'm sure that you have their full attention. Smile and offer them three free **Special Referral Gift Certificates.** Offer 3 to each single dinner or couple; you can give 3 extra ones if they are two couples having dinner together.

The amount for each gift certificate should be $25 or less if your menu prices are low. Ask them to give the gift certificates to three of their closest friends or family members, so that they can come over and try your place by themselves.

Tell them that because you really appreciate them doing this, you are also giving them a Gift Certificate for themselves, so that they come over again. Fill in, in front of them, these special gift certificates with their names.

Your clients would probably be thrilled that you give them something free (their own gift certificate), and they will be more than happy to get and pass along these additional three gift certificates. But there is one more reason for you to give this $25 to your current clients: it will make them come back and probably drag along some of their friends who otherwise could postpone going to your place and then eventually forget about it.

The reason why you should give them the 3 gift certificates for their friends and relatives is the geometrical growth that they will produce.

Think about it: If 10 clients get 3 gift certificates to pass along to their friends, this will bring 30 potential new clients assuming that the people who receive the gift certificates come along. Now, most likely they will bring along a friend, relative or significant other, increasing your number from 30 to 60.

And there is even potential for more people since many of them will come in groups of 4, making it possible to bring 120 new clients for just 10 of your clients passing along your gift certificates!

Now, we mentioned the Lifetime Value of a Client, remember? The value in our example was $2,400 but then you did your own homework to calculate how much a repeated client could potentially bring you in profit based on your own numbers.

If you can get 30 additional clients from these formal referrals, plus your 10 already clients that you gave the gift certificates to, this means that 40 clients will come to your place. Again, this is a conservative estimate, it could be many more.

Let's do some easy math:

- 40 clients: 30 new + 10 regulars that will come back with the gift certificates.

- Each Gift Certificate has a value of $25.

- For each of these $25 gift certificates, you'll pay $12 dollars. This is your cost in food per gift certificate.

- Your total cost for the 40 clients is $12 in food x 40 clients = $480 dollars invested.

- Your potential Return Of Investment (ROI) is = 40*$2,400= $96,000 potential dollars!

So for less than $500 dollars invested, you can get a potential $96,000 in profit. If this is not a worth it investment, I don't know what it is!

Again, you need to customize these numbers to match your own profit margins and food cost, but you get the idea.

I will show you the numbers in a simplified chart:

Since this Referral System will bring you very high quality people (after all, they would be family members and friends of your best clients), this $96,000 is a conservative number, and obviously much less than $480 dollars that you'll lose in food and beverage cost.

This is a very worth it investment for you to make.

Besides, because your place now offers excellence in service and food, these new people should be very happy to get a discount, and will probably spend some more than the $25 that they got, making this marketing investment even cheaper for you.

No other marketing investment will bring you results even close to these ones for the investment that you make!

5. Measure the Response and Repeat the Process

Make sure to track how many of these Referral Gift Certificates you give away and how many come back.

This will tell you if all, most of them, or only a few of the given gift certificates are being used. Remember our strategy? **Test and measure all you can!**

If you see many people coming with the special Referral Gift Certificates, then great, you know that the program is working.

If, on the other hand, you notice that not many of these special Gift certificates are coming back to you, then you should question if you gave the right amount of money, or if the clients that you selected were as good as you thought.

Try changing the amounts (raise the Referral Gift Certificates in amounts of $5 at a time, until you get your goal). Of course, don't expect people to come right away. You should wait a few months before they start showing up.

Sometimes their lives are busy or they have plans for the weekend or they just want to come together with the people who gave them the gift certificates and they don't find the right schedule to make it happen.

Whatever it is, just wait a few months before you start making any changes.

And keep in mind your worst-case scenario: if they don't come, you don't spend any money!

This is a risk free marketing and that's the beauty of this model. The downside is almost zero (just the cost of designing and printing the gift certificates), and the upside could mean thousands of dollars (or hundreds of thousands if you do your homework) in future revenues.

But, remember, it is very expensive to attract new clients. You should grow your business by doing more business with the clients that you already have.

Offer more of everything to these wonderful people who are already giving you their money: more menu or service choices, more price options, more extended services to accommodate their needs.

You should always keep their well-being and priorities on the top of your mind at all times. The reward will come to you a thousand fold.

In the next chapter, we will cover some strategies to increase the amount that your regular clients spend in your place.

H O M E W O R K

These are the 5 steps to calculate your Lifetime Value of a Client:

1. Calculate your average sale (from your sales records).

2. Calculate your average cost and profit per sale.

   For example, if your average sale per client is $30 (including food and drinks) and your average cost is $17, you are making a profit of $13 per client.

3. Calculate how much additional profit a client is worth to you by determining how many times he or she will come back. You can do this monthly or yearly but, remember, the average American moves every 5 years, so coming to your place once a month for 5 years should be a good estimate.

4. Double the number that you got in point 3. We mentioned that we assume people don't

come alone to dine, so assuming that they will bring at least one person with them is very realistic. Of course you will have the occasional lonely dinner, but there will be also groups of 3 or more so 2 is a fairly conservative number.

In this case, your Lifetime Value per client will be: $13 (your profit) * 12 (months) * 5 years * 2 people = $1,560

You can simplify this formula as follows:

$$\textbf{LTVC} = \textit{YPC} * \textbf{120}$$

- LTVC = Lifetime Value of One Client

- YPC = Your Profit per Client (you need to enter the value here after you calculated your own as mentioned in points number 1 and 2)

- 120 (Average Constant) = 12 months * 5 years * 2 clients

LTVC is your Lifetime Value of One of Your Clients.

Chapter 9:
Increasing Purchase Amount

You owe it to your clients to give them more of the best

We covered in the previous chapter how to bring more people to your place who hopefully will become regular clients. Now we need to see what you can do to increase the amount of money that each one of them spends in your place.

There are 3 main ways to increase their purchase amount:

1. Increase the price of your menu items

2. Increase the number of menu items that you sell

3. Sell additional merchandise

I would add one more - although this one is more complicated to implement - if you don't have it already:

4. Start/Promote a Catering Business

Let's cover each one in detail.

1.- Increase the Price of Your Menu Items

I suggested that you change your menu prices and test the new prices until you reach the perfect price for your items. The perfect price is the one that gives you the maximum amount of profit while still maintaining sales levels. Please go back to Chapter 5 and reread the section called **Test Your Marketing.**

Once you are comfortable with your prices, I recommend that you increase your menu prices annually (perhaps at the beginning of the year - on January 2nd) to compensate for the rising cost of living and the erosion of your profit because of inflation.

However, please keep in mind that you need to solidify your client base first and make sure that your regular clients are not overly price-sensitive. The referrals method that we've covered in Chapter 8 is a great way to capture high-quality clients.

Would you have any other reason to increase your menu prices? The answer is **absolutely**.

If you've followed my recommendations and started really caring about your clients - if your place is beautiful, your food excellent and your service impeccable - your place will soon become very popular (to the point where people will have to make reservations well in advance to secure a table.

Raising your prices in this case makes sense, since you will eliminate some clients who are more sensitive to high prices while still retaining enough clientele who can afford dining at your wonderful place.

You owe it to your best clients to give them the quality dining experience that they deserve, and if this means raising the prices so that you can compensate a tremendous staff and buy high quality products for your menu, so be it.

2.- Increase the Number of Menu Items That You Sell.

This means promoting additional sales. Here are some examples of extra sales that you can make:

* **Mineral Water:** are you offering your clients a good quality mineral water? Very often, if you fill

your client's glasses with tap water they will drink it without even considering ordering a mineral water bottle. Get some good mineral water from your distributors and ask your servers to offer it every single time that somebody sits at your tables. You will be surprised how many times the clients will gladly accept it and you will get an extra profit.

- **Degustation Menu:** Do you have a special, exclusive, high-end degustation menu? If not, you should. Create (together with your chef) a pre-set optional menu with dishes not found in your normal menu. You can call it something like '*Your Restaurant Name' Degustation Menu.* If your menu is attractive (one nice appetizer, two small portion entrées, a special dessert and a choice of nice complementary wines), many people will order it.

  People who come to your place for special occasions (birthdays, celebrations, romantic dates, etc.) or corporate types whose company pays the bill will very often order a special menu if you make it attractive enough. After all, this can be a special, unique choice, and they won't feel like they are getting pressured even if the price is high.

  Just make sure that you clearly put the price in the menu so that there are no surprises.

- **Limited Availability Wines or Beers:** Talk to your wine or beer distributors and get a special batch of a very good wine or specialty beers, then announce to your staff and clients that this wine is available only for a week and that it won't be found anywhere else. This highlights a limited edition and many clients, who normally wouldn't order wine, may ask for this one.

  NOTE: Please make sure that the wine is not available in supermarkets or local wine stores - or your credibility will be damaged.

- **Special Cocktails:** If you have a full bar, ask your barman to create some exotic cocktails that are not well known. Customize them and give them funny and easy-to-order names. If you don't have a full bar but still serve cocktails, you can research special drinks by going online and searching (in Google, MSN LiveSearch or Yahoo) for cocktails. There is a ton of information available.

  Then create a cocktail menu (make it nice and classy), and display it on your tables or ask your servers to give it to the people as they sit). Cocktails can make you a really good profit and women like them, especially when they go out in groups.

- **Small Portion Desserts:** I know that this sounds silly but oftentimes big desserts are a bad idea.

Think about it, people order dessert at the end of the meal when they are already full and feel guilty about the calories that they've just ingested. However, they would probably still want to taste something sweet, but humongous mud pies or chocolate cakes that are often offered as desserts are not what they have in mind.

If, on the other hand, you offer them small portions of high quality tarts, mousses and sorbets, not only your profit margin will improve but you'll also sell more of these since people won't feel as guilty ordering small portions of a sweet treat.

It is a good idea to create a variety sample tray of different desserts. This will be very attractive for parties, since there is always somebody with a sweet tooth, and if the portions are small it will entice the rest of the party to try something as well.

- **Offer some free tasty food to your wine or cocktail drinkers:** This is a simple but effective strategy to promote a glass of wine or a cocktail.

Create a featured small appetizer such as some roasted almonds, marinated olives, roasted bell peppers, etc. (or any other very small dish appropriate for the kind of food that you serve in your place) and serve it with a nice presentation to the people who order a glass of wine or a cocktail.

They will be greatly surprised, and some people will order the drink to receive the special treat. It shouldn't cost you much to do this.

Very soon word of mouth will spread and you'll start selling more servings of wines or cocktails than you expected. As an additional bonus, make these foods salty thereby inviting people to order another drink.

3.- Sell Additional Merchandise

Other than the food that you serve and the drinks that you pour, what else can you sell in your restaurant? A restaurant is a wonderful place because it gives you lots of opportunities for selling extra items to clients who are having a great time and already spending time at your place. These are some of the items that you could also offer for sale in your place to increase your profit:

- **Conserves & Preserves:** Do you have a dish that you could package, paste a label with your logo and the restaurant name, and sell to your clients?

Some foods that you could be converted into preserves are: roasted peppers, pickles, zucchini, pearl onions, garlic and other vegetables or fruits like strawberries, peaches, etc.

You could also create spreads (fish and some meats would be good candidates for them).

- **Third party food products:** Similar to the previous idea but this time you don't need to do the work, just sell somebody else's products.

Do you know some local farmer or businessperson who sells high-quality homemade preserves or conserves similar to the food that you sell?

If not, you can try to find them online - or ask your providers.

Many times your vendors may know some small entrepreneur who has approached them (or their managers) to distribute their products.

Often the big distributors won't carry these products, not because of their lack of quality (they are usually really good), but because of the small amounts that the providers can produce.

However, this is not a problem for a small place like yours.

Once you select the appropriated product/partner, contact them and offer to sell their products in your place.

You will sell the products for them, and they will be responsible for routine inventory checks and restocking to make sure that you always have inventory available (from time to time you may have to call them if you see that you are running low).

Then you can split the profits 50/50.

This is a great way to increase your profit per client since you don't have to do anything.

Your only job is to select a high quality product, contact the maker and then negotiate the agreement. After that, everything is gravy for you.

And by the way, this can also work with products from your distributors. Perhaps they have some products that people order frequently or perhaps ingredients that are too expensive for you to incorporate in your dishes but they will be great to put in a fancy container and sell them in small portions with a big markup.

Always check what products your distributors have available that could be divided and sold in small portions.

Also, again, please listen to your clients. They will tell you what they really like. If you are attentive to their tastes and interests, you can find new sales opportunities.

- **Exotic Oils:** Buy Extra Virgin Olive Oil from your distributors and some nice glass containers or bottles from an Import/Export shop or department store. Add some fresh spices to the oil (you can get some great recipes here: http://www.oliveoilsource.com/flavoring_olive_oils.ht m). Decorate the bottles with a ribbon or a nice rope around the neck of the jar or bottle, and add a label with your logo.

- **Recipe Books:** I'm sure that you have some great recipes on your menu. Why don't you share them with your clients? You could create a book by writing down your recipes and hiring a photographer to take some shots of your dishes.

Once you have all the necessary pieces packaged, you can go to websites such as www.blurb.com to list your products. There are also other sites such as www.booksurge.com (part of Amazon.com) or www.lulu.com where not only can you create beautiful books that you can display and sell in your restaurant, but you can also sell them online at no cost to you.

They will print and deliver the books only when people request them. You set your markup over the printing cost and keep the difference.

If you don't want the books to be so expensive, you can still create the books in a program such as Microsoft Word or Publisher and bring the files to Kinko's (www.fedexkinkos.com) to create books with bindings.

Not only can you make some extra money, but you can also have a reminder of your restaurant in the homes of your clients. Their friends will see your book and ask about your place. This will also give your restaurant more credibility and status with the local community, press, etc.

And remember, you can always trade (barter) some gift certificates as a payment for the work to a local printer or to a student who knows how to do desktop publishing. You don't need to do all of this by yourself.

- **Cooking Classes:** You could organize some cooking classes using the downtime in your restaurant.

  For example, do you open on Saturdays and/or Sundays for lunch? If not, these could be great days to organize the cooking classes.

You could teach them yourself if you like teaching and cooking, or ask your chef to put together some of your simpler dishes that your clients could learn how to cook.

Don't worry about teaching your secrets. Even if they learn how to make some of your dishes, they will always appreciate coming to your place and trying the real thing or they can just order something else.

This could also increase your potential market since cooking classes are often popular for corporate morale events, birthday parties and other group activities.

- **Sauces:** Similar idea to the conserves and preserves. Do you have some special or unique sauce that you use in your dishes? If so, you may want to can it or put it in a nice jar and sell it.

- **Spice Mixes:** For some restaurants, this could be a great way to sell the spices that you sell in some of your dishes, conveniently mixed and pre-packaged. The advantage of selling spices is that they stay fresh for a long time. You can create some nice looking cloth bags and tie them with some ribbons to make them attractive to your clients.

- **Food to Go:** It sounds cheap, but it doesn't have to be. Sometimes people, for whatever reason (a sick family member or friend, movie night at home, etc.) want to have great food but can't or don't want to dine in your restaurant.

  Give them the choice to call in advance and stop by your place to pick up their food. You should have some nice containers and paper bags (again with your logo and name) to place the food so that they can take it to go.

  Here is an idea for you: Why don't you buy a few nice picnic baskets (yes, the ones that they sell for trips to the park) and use them for carry-out orders?

  Not only this will be a touch of class, but also they will be greatly surprised with the idea. You can pack the food neatly inside Tupperware containers and even have space for a bottle of wine if they want to order one.

  Ask them to return the basket the next day or a few days later. In this way, they will have to come back to your place and - who knows - they may stay for dinner!

http://www.myrestaurantmarketing.com

You can decorate the picnic baskets with your logo so that there is no question that they belong to your business.

In any case, the word will spread very fast and soon you will see many clients ordering food from your place to have the "picnic basket experience".

This is just one more way for you to differentiate from your competitors.

And here is another idea for you: What about if you make a barter deal with some local merchant who sells these picnic baskets whereby you can get them in exchange for gift certificates? Always trying bartering when we can :-)

Or at least ask for a discount in exchange for including the merchant's flyer in the basket (advertising it) every time that you stuff it with your food.

- **Sell Goods:** Make a deal with a local jewelry designer and ask her for merchandise to display at your restaurant. You can set up a nice looking shelf or table and display the jewelry for all your customers and clients to see. You can get a commission on any sales that the sale of the merchandise generates.

You could even be more daring and ask the designer to model her jewelry (or hire a professional model to do it) going from table to table in your dining room. I saw this done in an upscale restaurant with great success. Their clients love this idea.

If you feel uneasy about alienating your clients by doing this, just ask some of your best and regular clients what they think about this idea. You will get honest and valuable feedback and they may like it if there is no sales pressure involved.

- **Sell Art:** Ask local artists to exhibit their best paintings or sculptures in your place. Hang them in appropriate locations with a clear label with titles, descriptions and prices.

  You can take care of the transaction (sale) and get a percentage of any generated sales.

  You can agree with the artists to rotate the art pieces once every three months or so. In this way, you move the art that doesn't sell and get new art in your walls.

  Not only this will help you increase your revenue, but also your place will always be decorated with beautiful art that will greatly contribute to your ambience.

Your clients will appreciate going to dinner in a place exhibiting beautiful pieces of art!

- **Sell Background Music:** Find local musicians that match your ambience and restaurant. If people like the music and ask you about it, you can always have some CDs for sale. Not only can you get some commissions from the sales of the CDs, but your place will also have some original music that people won't find anywhere else.

4.- Start/Promote a Catering Business

I won't go into much detail here since the catering business, because of its peculiarities, will require a whole book to explain the topic.

The idea is simple but I know that the implementation can be complicated.

In any case - here goes: since you have the equipment, the food, the business and operations experience, advertisement media (your own restaurant, your website, etc.), why don't you expand your business and create a catering unit that can expand your sales?

This could be a great revenue generator, especially in the summertime or holiday periods when people often host parties at their houses, churches, community centers, etc.

Many of your own clients will probably be interested in having you (their trusted food expert and friend) catering their events or will recommend you to their friends, church members, relatives, colleagues, business associates, etc.

Think about it. You know your staff's schedule better than anybody.

Do you have weaker, seasonal times where you could complement your restaurant sales with offsite catering?

Do you have the staff (or can you train temporary staff) to serve your clients with the same level of quality and excellence that they expect from you?

If so, create a catering menu. Add a catering page to your restaurant website. Create catering business cards and small fliers that you can put on your tables.

Tell your clients about your plans to start a catering business. Analyze their comments; see how they respond to your idea. You will get a feel for how this new business concept resonates with them.

If you already have a catering business: Are you doing all you can to promote it in your restaurant?

Are you telling your restaurant clients about it?

A good idea is to give your current clients a voucher for a 10% or 15% discount for any catered event that they may want, valid for one year.

Don't put their name in the voucher so that they can give it to their friends, family members or colleagues. This is a great way to start generating the business.

Also, are you aware that you can apply many of the lessons from this book to your catering business?

- Excellence in service

- Really caring about the interest of your clients

- Creating a USP

- Etc.

Just go over the materials and think how you can extrapolate many of the thoughts, ideas and concepts to your catering business.

By now, you know much more about marketing, and you can apply this knowledge to any other business that you may want to start.

In the end please keep your clients' satisfaction and dining experience in mind at all times. Don't try to create so many up-selling systems that you alienate your clients and make them feel added sales pressure.

Start slowly. Implement one or two of these ideas at a time and always - always - ask for feedback from your clients. They will tell you what they like and what they don't.

As you can see, implementing these strategies to increase the purchase amount per client is more cost-effective for you than trying to capture new clients.

Since you already have the people sitting in your place, you can talk to them and ask them for feedback.

You will be surprised how many of these ideas will be welcomed by your clientele, and not only will they increase your profit and sales per client, but will also make your restaurant unique and different from your competitors.

In our next and final chapter (Chapter 10) we will talk about how to increase the frequency of visits from your current clients.

H O M E W O R K

Brainstorm and create a list with:

- **Additional menu items** that you could offer to your clients (you can include some or all of the suggested ideas plus some that you can think of yourself).

- **Additional merchandise** that you can sell in your place (same as above: you can use my list and/or add some more items from your own ideas).

- **Do you have a Catering Business?**

  NO→Are you thinking about starting one?

  YES→ Are you using your restaurant as a marketing platform?

  Will you use this book and apply the learning that you got into your Catering Business?

Chapter 10:
Increasing Frequency of Visits

Bring back your best clients over and over.

So you've attracted many new people to your place by implementing the strategies that we discussed in Chapter 8. You've also increased the purchase amount per client by following the techniques from Chapter 9.

Now we want to bring these higher yielding clients (they should be your *clients* by now) more times to your restaurant.

In this chapter, we will discuss several proven strategies that won't cost you too much to implement - and they work like a charm. Remember that the most costly marketing objective (and often the most used by your competitors) is the one designed to bring new people to your place.

However, you know better by now. Your current clients know about your place, they like it and like your food and your service. It's logical that you should spend some time and effort to make sure they don't forget about you.

3 reasons why a client may stop going to your restaurant

There are three main reasons why clients may stop going to your restaurant:

1. They moved out of town or to a new place far away and your restaurant is not convenient for them anymore.

2. They were unhappy the last time that they went to your restaurant but they never told you.

3. They just are too busy and forgot about you, or sometimes they remember your restaurant but they keep on postponing going to your place.

We will cover later in this chapter what you can do to solve problems two and three (there is not much that we can do about number one). But before you can bring your clients back, you need to know who they are.

Certainly you may recognize your clients when you see them. You may even know some first or last names for some of them. But **do you know how to contact them?**

How to Bring Back Your Clients:

Gathering client information is the first step that you need to master to be successful in bringing your clients back:

You need to setup a system to capture your clients' information. The more information you can gather without being intrusive or violating a client's privacy, the better off you'll be.

Remember, you want to establish a personal relationship with your clients. You really want to care about them, about their lives, their families.

This should be a natural process. If you talk to them when they visit your place, if you ask them with genuine interest about their families, their lives; they will be honored and happy to share it with you.

Start creating a database with their information in your computer.

If you don't have a computer, don't panic. You can still create a database by hand on 3" x 5" index cards, and then ask someone on your staff to enter the data into a computer. You can also outsource this task to a student or a company who can do it for you.

You need to have this information stored digitally because you'll use it later to send postcards, coupons, newsletter emails and other reminders to your clients.

By the way, if you don't have a computer, you should seriously consider getting one. Also get some basic computer training at a local Community College or through an adult education programs or by private tutoring with a computer-savvy person. Training shouldn't cost you much, and there are so many things that you can do with a computer to improve your marketing that training is totally worth the investment!

I would recommend that you get a laptop. This way you can carry it with you and work at home, at your restaurant or pretty much anywhere where there is an outlet and a seat.

RECOMMENDED SOFTWARE TO TRACK YOUR CLIENTS

An application like Microsoft Excel (part of the Microsoft Office Suite) will allow you to easily keep track of all the information that you need.

If you have a Mac, you can also buy iWorks for $79 (the Basic Office for Mac will cost you around $130).

iWorks for Mac is like an Office light and would be enough for you to keep track of your clients with the application called Numbers (similar to Microsoft Excel).

The Windows version is a little more expensive (around $180).

I would recommend you get a copy of Office, since you will be using the software for many other tasks like mail merge, writing invoices, memos, letters, etc. This investment is not that expensive and it's totally worth it, since you will be using these functions over and over.

However, if you don't want to spend any money buying software, you can also download a free version of a Microsoft Office-compatible application called Open Office.

You can download it here: http://openoffice.org-suite.com/index.asp?aff=101

Open Office is an open source program (meaning that many people work and contribute to the development of this software free of charge) that offers similar functionality to Microsoft Office. The downside is that it is not as polished or totally compatible with Microsoft Office so you may run into problems if you are exchanging files with your printer, other people, etc.

You may want to give it a try and see if it works for you.

If you have a high-speed Internet connection you don't even need to buy iWorks or Office since there are free online applications that can get the work done.

The only downside of these applications is that you need to be online (connected) all the time to work with them.

Some applications for you to check out are:

- Microsoft Office Live for Small Business: http://smallbusiness.officelive.com/ Microsoft has a great offering for small businesses like yours. You'll get everything you need to create a professional online presence, including free Web hosting, easy-to-use site design tools, site traffic reports, and more. Check the entire offering in their web site.

- Edit Grid: www.editgrid.com

- Think Free: www.thinkfree.com

- Google Docs: www.docs.google.com/#

- Other office-like web services: www.zoho.com (Zoho also has an online database. You can import your contacts from Excel). Mac users can also use Bento ($49)

- Another alternative is www.Catalystweb.com (integrated office applications + email, calendar & contacts). This one costs $25/month for 10 GB of storage (enough for an average restaurant)

- Etc.

I've created a simple Excel template that you can download and use to capture your clients' information. It is free for all of you that have purchased my book. Just go to my website: ww.myrestaurantmarketing.com/book/links.html to download it.

Basically, you need to capture the following items for each person:

- Last Name:

- First Name:

- Birthday:

- Spouse Name:

- Spouse Birthday:

- Address:

- City:

- ZIP:

- Phone Number:

- Email:

- Frequency of Visits:

- Inactive Client? (Y/N):

- Preferred Client? (Y/N):

- Notes:

Although Excel will get the job done (it has some database capability built in), there are other tools better designed to manage your clients.

They are called Customer Relationship Management Tools (or CRM).

CUSTOMER RELATIONSHIP MANAGEMENT TOOLS (CRM)

These are sophisticated software tools that can help you track your most loyal restaurant clients.

CRM tools provide you with several integrated chapters as follows:

- **Contacts:** Here is where you store the data about your clients: name, address, emails, phone numbers, birthdays, etc.

- **Groups:** You can make groups of your contacts (for example categorize your clients by professions, by location, by spending habits, etc.)

- **Calendar:** The calendar allows you to setup alarms when you need to take action (for example, you can use it to enter general reminders such as when you need to mail your newsletter, update your web site, etc.) or individual reminders per client (for example, a reminder of upcoming birthdays so that you can mail them gift certificates or reminders for following up with phone calls), etc.

- **Appointments:** You can also keep track of your personal appointments here (with your providers, marketing contacts, maintenance, financial, etc.)

- **Tasks:** It allows you to keep track of your daily, weekly or monthly tasks so that you don't forget.

- **Notes:** You can add notes to all of the above.

- **Etc.**

These are just some examples of common functions that you can find in CRM programs.

Keeping in touch with your restaurant clients and encouraging repeat business is the first lesson in customer relationship management (CRM). If you want to give someone a call and can't remember what you spoke about last time, a CRM tool is invaluable.

If you are interested in learning more about CRM programs and you have a PC, I would recommend for you to check this web site that analyzes the best CRM programs for Windows: http://www.smallbizcrm.com/small-business-crm-crm-for-windows.html

Again, Microsoft also has a free CRM offering as part of their Office Live for Small Business. You can find it here: http://smallbusiness. officelive.com/Manage/ContactManager/

If you run your business with a Mac, you can find some (though there are less offers than for Windows) here: http://www.smallbizcrm.com/crm-apple-macintosh.html

Ok, so how do you gather all this information?

There are several ways to populate your database.

The most obvious and easy way is to get some data when your clients make reservations.

Ask your servers to capture the last and first name and the phone number every time that somebody calls to make a reservation. This is a common practice and it will also help you to find the person in case they forget something at your place, etc.

So, go back to your reservations book or reservations software and start entering the information in the template that I gave you (or ask someone on your staff to do the job for you).

You will need to get the rest of the information: spouse name, both dates of birth, address and email directly from your clients.

STEP-BY-STEP SYSTEM TO GET INFORMATION FROM YOUR CLIENTS:

1. Approach your clients and tell them that you are starting a new program. Tell them you'd like to send them a complimentary gift certificate for their birthdays (we will cover this strategy in more detail later in the chapter) and that you are doing this only for your best clients.

   They should feel happy, honored and willing to give you this information.

2. Create some small cards (you can get them from a local printer or a FedEx-Kinko's office) with the fields that you need.

3. Pre-populate these cards with the all the information that you already know about your clients (probably their name and phone number at this point; perhaps also the name of their spouse).

4. Ask them to help you fill in the rest of the data.

   WARNING: Please notice that the following fields: **Frequency of Visits, Inactive Clients, Preferred Clients** and **Notes** are for your eyes only and shouldn't be displayed on the cards that you'll give to your customers.

5. Once you've captured this information, ask your clients if they would also like to receive (via email) a newsletter from you as well as some coupons or other interesting information about your place.

6. Promise them that you won't be spamming them with email (contacting them no more than once a month) and that they can unsubscribe anytime they like. Also tell them that your strict policy is that you will never share their information with any other third party.

7. If you see that they are uneasy about giving you their email addresses then don't capture their email information. You can always communicate with them via regular mail or by calling them, if necessary.

*This system can be uncomfortable but it is
essential to bring clients back to your place over
and over!*

Now you are working hard capturing your clients'
information or delegating this task to some of your
trusted employees.

Very Important: Start with your best clients and add
more customers once you feel comfortable with this
process.

You want to capture as many clients as possible to
convert them into repeated clients.

*Remember, this system will cost you less and will
bring more money than any other marketing
method.*

What do we do with our client's information?

So, you ask, what do we do with all this information?

Glad you asked.

We do have several great mechanisms to make people think about your place and pick up the phone to make reservations. Let's look at some of them:

1. CALL YOUR FORMER CUSTOMERS IF YOU HAVE THEIR PHONE NUMBER:

This is very important to re-activate dormant clients. There are several steps involved in this process:

1. COLLECT DATA:

Go over your reservation books or software and look back for one year

How many clients used to come to your place but have not returned recently

Write down their names and phone numbers, then one rainy afternoon (OK, it doesn't need to be rainy but it will give you the opportunity when it is slow) start calling them.

2. CONTACT THEM:

Tell them that you were looking at your client list and you saw that they have not visited in awhile. Ask them if there was something wrong with their last visit. Apologize if you failed to give them the experience that they deserved and listen for their explanation.

Remember what we covered before? Most likely they will tell you one of the three reasons why they are not coming anymore:

2.1 They have moved away:

    a. If they really moved far away then tell them that you miss them and that, if they ever come back to visit, you will be glad to see them again in your place, then thank them for their time and delete them from your list.

2.2 They were not satisfied with their last visit(s):

    b. Tell them that you are implementing new policies, that you have dramatically improved your service and that you would love for them to come back and check your place again.

    c. Tell them that you are so sure that they will love your place that you would like to mail them a gift certificate for $50 so that they can have dinner at your place.

2.3 Nothing special happened, they just forgot about you:

You may want to give them a $25 gift certificate to bring old clients back if they tell you that they were happy with you and they have just postponed a visit or forgot about your establishment. Don't get too cheap. Remember the value of a repeat client for your business; they could be worth potentially thousands of dollars to you.

You should do anything possible to bring your clients back, even if it's at no profit or a small loss. Consider this effort as an investment.

3. UPDATE THEIR ADDRESS:

Most likely, your former clients will react very positively to your offer and will give you their address.

This will also give you one more piece of information for your database. Reassure your clients that you will be mailing this gift certificate soon, (and of course, follow up and do it right away), and let them know that you hope to see them at your place.

Make sure that you note in your database that they were inactive clients who are coming back again.

NOTE: I've created an Excel Template that you can use to track your clients. You can download the Excel template Clients Database.xls from my website: www.myrestaurantmarketing.com (you'll need to subscribe to get access to the download area)

I've added a field called "Inactive Clients Y/N" to flag the clients that you have re-activated.

2. GIVE THEM SPECIAL TREATMENT:

Now, it is very important that they get special treatment when they come in so they will change their minds about your place, especially if they left with a bad taste last time, but it is also logistically difficult for your staff to remember who was who when they come.

How can you make sure that your staff knows that these are special clients that you want to pamper and treat with great care? You could add a note in the database, but this is too complicated to manage.

There is a much simpler solution that I will share with you: Create special gift certificates unique for former clients (perhaps with a special logo, a special color that you don't normally use, or just simply printing **Former Client Gift Certificate** in the heading, or any other coding that is easy to remember for you and your staff.

This way your staff doesn't have to remember anything; they'll just have to collect these special gift certificates. By the way, when you tell your former clients that you are mailing them gift certificates, remember to tell them that they should redeem the gift certificate with their server as soon as they cross your door, so that they can get special VIP treatment.

By doing this you easily identify former clients that you are trying to bring back. If they leave your place really happy with their experience, they will probably come back again and again.

3. SEND THEM BIRTHDAY CERTIFICATES:

Yes, we're discussing more gift certificates but bear with me. These will really work for you. I'll explain the Why, How, When and Who of this marketing technique. Let's look at each one now:

Why?

Remember what I told you about capturing clients' information?

A good reason to collect your client's information - and a reason that nobody will question you - is to tell them that you will be mailing a gift card as a present for their birthday and a token of your appreciation of their business.

How?

Enter the dates in the database and also in an electronic calendar.

Again, if you have Microsoft Office you can do this in the Calendar application, or in Entourage or iCal if you use a Mac, but there are other online applications that allow you to do this as well, such as:

- **Google Calendar:**
  http://www.google.com/calendar/

- **Yahoo Calendar:**
  http://calendar.yahoo.com/

- **Others:** You can find many more online calendars here: http://mashable.com /2007/10/08/online-calendar-toolbox

When?

Make sure that you set a reminder for yourself one month before a client's birthday.

Send them a nice postcard with a gift certificate made to the name of the birthday person (so that they can't give to anybody else) and valid for 10 days before through 10 days after their birthday only for an amount of $25 or $30. This gives them 20 days to honor the gift certificate, in case that they can't make it on that day.

Tell them how much you appreciate their patronage and how much you would like them to come to your place to celebrate such a special day.

Who?

Think about this. Even if you offer a $30 incentive, do you think these people will come alone to celebrate their birthday?

They will most likely bring along their spouses, and probably some other friends and family members.

Your $30 offer will probably be only a part of the hundreds of dollars the party will spend, and will make a very happy birthday person.

This is the stuff that we're talking about.

You really care about these people coming to your place. You know that their birthday is a very important occasion, and you also know that you can deliver the best available service and food. They deserve it - they should come to your place because they won't receive the special service at any other restaurant in the area.

As a bonus, you benefit from the others in the dining party since you can also get their friends and families' email addresses and other information - and everybody wins!

4. TELL TEM ABOUT SPECIAL EVENTS:

Sometimes people stop going to your place because they want something different. They are happy with your place and your food but, if they go too often, it will seem like the "same old same old". What can you do to attract these clients? You can host Special Events.

By offering something special, and communicating this to your current clients, you'll introduce some novelty to your place and will bring back some bored clients. These are just some suggestions of the kind of events you may host:

Wine dinners:

Do you serve wine? Then host a monthly wine dinner.

Work with your wine distributors and select exciting wines, pair them with a special menu, and tell all your clients about it (this is why it is so important for you to keep a database with your clients' contact information).

Because you'll be serving special wines and special food, this will be something interesting and exciting for your clients. This could also be a great opportunity for you to introduce and test new menu items and new wines.

Ask your clients how they like your special offerings; take note of their comments. This is also a great way for your clients to try new wines and learn about them, and because you'll manage the food/wine pairing, you eliminate the risk of your client not choosing the right wines.

Live Music:

People are attracted to music; it is in our genes. Bring some musicians (even if your place is small there may be space for a solo player) and let everybody know that one night a week (or biweekly, depending how often you want to do it) you'll have live music.

Please keep in mind that the volume shouldn't be too loud. Diners may still want to have a dinner and conversation.

When people enter your restaurant, ask them if they want to sit close to the musicians or far away from them. This way you give them the choice to either be close to the action or to sit in a quiet area and have the chance to talk.

Also, offer music that is appropriate for your place. If you have a restaurant with romantic ambience, a heavy metal band won't be very attractive to your clients - even if you personally love heavy metal.

Announce your live music selection on your website and/or newsletter, if you have one. It is a good idea to change musicians often since this will create a "one time opportunity" for people to listen to them. Your clients will feel motivated to go to your restaurant for fear of losing the chance to see and hear these musicians.

If you have the same music, band or ensemble night after night, people won't feel pressured to go to dinner at your restaurant because they know that they can catch that musician again at a future date.

You can schedule the music for a slow day of the week. If you can get quality music at a reasonable price (and even try to barter part of their fee by trading with gift certificates with the musicians), and advertise it to increase awareness, you should be able to increase the number of people coming to your place filling those empty tables.

But there is an extra perk. You can also make a deal with the musicians to sell their CDs (if they have them) to your clientele the day that they play the music. You don't need to actively do the selling. Just place the CDs in a visible place with the price on them and your interested clients will do the buying for you.

Remember, dining at a restaurant is an emotional experience so chances are that if people like the music, they will feel motivated to buy the CDs.

Split the profits 50/50 with the musician.

Poetry Reading:

I know, it sounds funny but this could be a good idea if you implement it correctly.

First contact a local poet. You could find them in the University Literary Clubs, or by going online to Google, MSN or Yahoo and entering "YOURCITY Poets" (where of course YOURCITY is the name of the city where your restaurant is located, or the closest big city nearby).

Usually poets love to be heard and you can probably get them to read their poems by simply offering them a free dinner.

Please make sure that you screen and approve the poems that they will be reading before they appear in front of your clients. You don't want to upset your clients with some offbeat poems that could offend diners or discuss topics of questionable taste.

You may want to talk to your clients before organizing the poetry reading, and ask them how do they feel about it and if they would enjoy it. If you get good response, then do it. It is very cheap for you to organize and it will give your place an aura of uniqueness and prestige.

If, on the other hand, you feel that the reaction of your clients is lukewarm at best, then just scrap the idea and move on with something else.

Profession-Specific Events:

You can target specialized professionals such as lawyers, accountants, IT pros, etc.

You can position your place as "The Lawyers on Tuesdays", or "The Doctors on Thursdays' Restaurant" and host special events (once a month or so) when the professionals in an industry get a discount and can mingle and network among themselves.

It is very easy to get their names and addresses (just look in the yellow pages) to create a mailing postcard with a coupon announcing the event and giving them a discount as incentive for them to come to your restaurant.

They will love it.

Charitable Dinners:

If you feel strong about a good cause, why not combine your business and your passion?

Host a charitable dinner and tell all your clients about it. Tell them that you will donate 10% of all the profits from the dinner to your favorite charity.

Most people will like the idea of contributing to charity by having a great meal and will come to your place. Also they will be impressed with your involvement in the community.

This is a win/win situation since you will still make money and will keep your place fresh in the minds of your clients.

Also, because it's for a good cause, you can probably get very good deals on advertising from local radio stations and newspapers.

Offer gift certificates to the dinner in exchange for free advertising, or even better suggest an interview to promote your cause or at least to announce it for free. Many local newspapers and radio stations are always looking for news and, since this event is for charity, they will feel good about telling their listeners or readers.

You can also create a press release, send it to all your local newspapers, and post it for free in places like http://www.free-press-release.com/, www.freepress.net, etc. (Again, you can just do a search for "Free Press Release" and you'll find a bunch of press release providers.)

Also, don't forget to post this event on your website and create flyers that you can give to the people going to your place. And to top it off, you can get some tax deductions (please consult with your accountant about this).

5. OFFER THEM PROMOTIONS:

Once in a while it is a good idea to create a promotion to introduce a new menu item, a new line of foods, your catering services, new wines, etc.

Promotions are good excuses for you to invite your clients to your place. Make an incentive out of it. Give them some coupons or discounts (this is the same idea as a Happy Hour for bars) so that they feel compelled to visit your place.

Also, use promotions to fill in the weakest days of the week. It is better to keep your place fresh in the minds your clients, even if you don't make too much money, than to have your restaurant empty some days.

Advertise your promotions on your website and in your newsletters

6. SEND THEM NEWSLETTERS:

Electronic or printed newsletters are a great way to keep your restaurant in the minds and hearts of your clients.

So what can you write about in your newsletter? Basically you need to talk about things that your readers (your clients) could find interesting.

These are some ideas for you to write about:

- Announce any event that will happen in your place (from the list that we just mentioned or any other event that you came up with on your own).

- Feature every month one of your employees so that people who go to your place can remember their names and feel like they know them.

- Explain about the area/region/country that defines your food and wine offerings.

- Add one recipe (this is a great way to start writing down your recipes and later create a recipe book that you can sell, as we discussed in Chapter 9).

- Add a good joke (everybody likes a good joke). You can find restaurant-themed jokes online by searching for them. Please keep them tasteful.

- Describe and explain one of your wines or special cocktails.

- Tell an interesting story that happened in your restaurant (for privacy purposes you should change the names of the people involved).

- Write about nutrition.

- Etc.

So you can see that newsletters are just vehicles to communicate with your clients. This is a great tool for you to entertain while you keep your place fresh in their minds.

However, don't use the newsletter to promote yourself. Keep the interests of your clients first and avoid shameless self-promotion. Consider that the more interesting and useful information you provide, the more likely your readers will find something interesting for them.

How often should you publish? I would recommend you to start quarterly to develop a reading habit among your clients. Six to eight times is better; eventually you should aim for monthly publication.

The design of your newsletter is very important.

I would recommend that you hire a graphic artist to design the look and feel of your newsletter (template) in a program that you can edit yourself later (such as Microsoft Publisher or Page Maker if you want to get fancy. Microsoft Word or Mac Pages can often "fit the bill").

It is worth it to invest some money to create an attractive and easy to read format. Keep in mind that people will judge your place based on the newsletter that they receive.

If the newsletter is sloppy, with poor design and/or content, it will reflect a poor image of your restaurant.

Now, we talked about printed and electronic newsletters. Which one is right for you?

Both have pros and cons. Let's quickly examine them:

Printed Newsletter

- **PROS:**

  o You can distribute them in hotels, apartment buildings, small businesses and office parks around your area, and create awareness of your place.

  o You can have them available in your restaurant so that people who are waiting can read them, etc.

  o You can mail them to your clients.

- o People like to read printed paper much more than a computer screen.

- **CONS:**

  - o They can be expensive to produce (depending how fancy you want to get with the paper type, color or black and white, etc.) and you'll need to pay postage when mailing.

  - o More labor intensive (you need to do folding, mailing or distribution, etc.).

  - o You may end up producing too many or too few newsletters than you need (this would eventually be fixed when you figure out after a few months how many issues you need to produce).

Electronic Newsletter

- **PROS:**

  - o They are very cheap to produce and distribute (development costs will be the same).

  - o Instant gratification: You can email them and your clients will get it right away.

- o You can post it on your website so that people who want hard copies can print them from there by themselves.

- o You'll never over- or under-produce since you know your mailing list and people who are not there can just download them and/or print them from your website.

- o Ecologically friendly since you won't be using any paper.

- **CONS:**

  - o Out of reach for some people who don't have email (such as older people).

  - o It could end up unread in the Junk Mail or deleted folder.

  - o More difficult to read online (although if you make it right, they should be able to print it if they choose to do so since it would be only a few pages long).

  - o Lack of distribution options, such as in businesses and hotels.

http://www.myrestaurantmarketing.com

So which one is right for you?

I would recommend a mixed model. Email the electronic version to people who give you their email address. Also, post it on your website.

Print a limited number of hard copies to distribute to hotels and businesses around your area. Keep several copies in the restaurant and mail a few to clients who request a copy.

This way you don't spend as much money in postage and printing since you won't give the printed copy to all your clients, you'll still keep a limited number of printed newsletters (around 100 or 200 should suffice) for the cases that we mentioned earlier.

And remember, newsletters are the ideal vehicle to communicate to your clients any special activities, events or promotions that you may be organizing in the coming weeks.

7. TELL THEM ABOUT YOUR WEBSITE:

You need to have an up-to-date, great looking website.

It is not a nice-to-have marketing vehicle but a must-have one!

http://www.myrestaurantmarketing.com

If you don't have a web site, please create one ASAP.

You don't need to have special skills; you don't need to create it yourself (actually, unless you're really good at designing, it's probably better that you don't do it yourself. A poorly designed website will do more damage than good to your business).

Just contact a Web design company (you can look at some recommended companies in the Resources page on my site www.MyRestaurantMarketing.com) and ask them to design an easy-to-maintain website for your restaurant.

Although many restaurants have a website, most of the restaurant sites are really lame, displaying only a couple of photos of their place and simply posting their phone number for people to make reservations.

A web presence should mean much more for restaurateurs than just showing some information.

The latest Internet usage statistics (June 2008,Nielsen//NetRatings) tell us that there are more than 220 million Internet users in the US. This represents 72.5% of the population, and means that most of your potential customers have access to the Internet.

And yet, most restaurateurs are doing next to nothing to promote their business online.

A website is a great vehicle for you to communicate with your existing and potential clients, so why are most restaurateurs not using their website more to do their online marketing?

There are probably several reasons, likely including the lack of technical knowledge and Internet experience of many restaurant owners. But having a solid web presence doesn't have to be difficult or complicated.

TEN ESSENTIAL WEBSITE REQUIREMENTS:

Your Web site must have the following requirements:

1. **Easy on the eye:**

   Nobody wants to look at ugly websites. However, don't choose form over substance. This is a mistake that many web masters/designers make.

   Just because they can use fancy flash intros,

with music and sophisticated graphics doesn't mean that these effects should be used. There is nothing more annoying than visiting a website looking for information only to suffer through a distracting and totally useless Flash movie.

Remember, your website is there to provide your clients with valuable information, **and to collect their information** so you can include them in your database. Any other uses are redundant.

2. **Simple:**

   You don't want to make it full of Java scripts and Flash animations. Not only will some clients with slower Internet connection be annoyed by how slow your website loads, but also Flash makes it more difficult for your site to be found by the main search engines.

3. **Easy to Navigate:**

   All the information on your site should be accessible and easy to find.

   Don't make your clients work hard to get the information that they're looking for.

If they go to your site, they want to get information quickly and painlessly. Make sure that your main categories (your menu, address, map to your site, phone number or online reservation system, etc.) are visible and easily accessible.

People have short attention spans, and will quickly abandon your site if they can't find the information that they need.

4. **Full of Interesting Content**:

Don't bore your clients with trivial information about how good your restaurant or your chef is. Instead, use it to inform them of any news, events, information, etc.

Post meaningful information often on your site to motivate people to visit it frequently and check out your updates. For example, you can announce special events that you are hosting, such as charity dinners, wine dinners, new menu items, etc.

Post your menus and your wine list online with your updated prices. This way, people won't get surprised when they see the price list when they visit.

5. **Accessible Contact Information**:

    Make it easy for people to reach you. Add your address and a map with directions to your place (this is easy; you can ask your web designer to add a link to Yahoo, Google or MSN maps).

    Post your phone number and email so that people can make reservations and reach you with comments or questions.

6. **Add Suggestions Box:**

    Encourage people to send you comments and suggestions about how to improve your place, how to make your clients' dining experience better. This will be invaluable feedback for you to understand what your clients want and like. The more you know your clients, the better you can provide them with a great experience.

7. **Easy to Update and Maintain:**

    There is nothing worse than an outdated site with old information. You can't rely on the people who created the web site to be making changes all the time (not only this would be terribly expensive, but also you will delay the information).

Learn how to use and maintain your site. You are the owner of the place; you need to also to own your website. For this reason, when you have your website designed, please make sure that it's designed so that you can easily update the content.

8. **Registration Form:**

You want your clients to be able to register their emails to be added to your distribution list so that they can receive your newsletters and other offers automatically.

This will save you a lot of work. This step is very important - since the more names and email addresses that you have from your clients, the more you can use this information to send messages with promotions, gift certificates, discount coupons and other announcements.

However, people don't like to give away their personal information, so you need to motivate them by giving something away in exchange for their contact information.
For example, you could use an opt-in form that says something like:
"Please enter your name and email in the form

below to receive a coupon for a free entrée (or a 15% discount, $20 gift certificate, etc.) so you can try our wonderful restaurant"

By the way, I've just found a tool that can help you tremendously to get more people subscribing to your list and therefore getting coupons and going to your restaurant. It is called Tell-a-Friend Software (or TAFPro for short).

This software (which - as of the time of this writing - costs $97) is an Automatic Referral System that will bring good quality referrals to your website. You can find more information here: http://www.tafpro.com/?15287

The beauty of this software is that you only pay the $97 once and then you can use it forever with your site to attract new clients by using the networking of people visiting your site.

Not only is this a great way to capture new clients, but the marketing cost for you is very small. If it doesn't work, you don't have any additional expenses. If it works, you have a potential client for life. There is no downside here.

You can also add an optional field for birthday,

where you capture ONLY the month and day (so people won't be afraid of divulging too much personal information). This will be really useful for you to use when sending the gift certificates or discount coupons (as we explained earlier) whenever a birthday is coming soon.

Not only will you attract the birthday guest, but they'll bring along friends and/or family as well, since birthdays are usually social events.

By the way, please don't give coupons away if people don't register. You want to capture as many names and emails as possible. The coupons are your way to make sure that they give you their names and email addresses.

Very Important: Enter the information that you've gathered in your restaurant directly on your website form (or ask a staff member to do it for you). By following this process, you assure that all the information is collected in the central database, and that they are legitimate email addresses following the opt-in process.

9. **Your Newsletter:**

Add your newsletter (if you have one) to your site, formatted so that it is easy to read and to print (if you clients prefer to read it on paper).

10. Interesting Photos, Videos, Recipes

You can post some videos and photos of your place, but remember: **don't post them on the main page**!

Some people like to know what to expect before they go to your restaurant, but they don't want to get annoyed if they have already been to your place and are looking only for specific information.

You can also post recipes or - even better - a short video with your chef cooking a signature dish. This will make your place unique and special.

You can also post these videos on YouTube with a link to your site increasing your exposure even more.

There are some other features that, although not as important as the ones covered earlier can also be very useful, such as:

• **Blog:**

Wikipedia defines blog as follows:

"A blog (a contraction of the term "web log") is a website, usually maintained by an individual, with regular entries of commentary, descriptions of events, or other material such as graphics or video. Entries are commonly displayed in reverse-chronological order. "Blog" can also be used as a verb, meaning to maintain or add content to a blog.

Many blogs provide commentary or news on a particular subject; others function as more personal online diaries. A typical blog combines text, images, and links to other blogs, web pages, and other media related to its topic. The ability for readers to leave comments in an interactive format is an important part of many blogs."

A blog could be an alternative to the newsletter as a way to have your clients informed of all the new things happening in your place.

It is fast, easy and a great way for you to communicate information to your clients without the need to update the content of your website.

You can combine blogs with RSS (these initials stand for Real Simple Syndication). It is just a fancy way to refer to a service used to publish frequently updated content such as blog entries or news headlines, where users subscribe and are automatically notified every time that you add new information.

RSS makes it possible for people to keep up with their favorite web sites in an automated manner rather than checking them manually. To find out more about RSS, just visit Wikipedia or Google the term "RSS". You will find a lot of information.

- **Online Reservations**

In addition to accepting reservations via phone, this is a very efficient way to receive and track reservations. Your clients will be able to make reservations even when there is no one available to pick up the phone at your restaurant, and you'll always be sure that the information is correct. How many times has a voice message been unclear or incomplete and you get the wrong information?!

When your clients book online, they are responsible for entering the correct information. One more advantage is that you can ask them to enter their email address (for new customers), increasing the size of your list.

There are companies such as OpenTable who offer online registration services.

They will put a terminal in your restaurant where you'll see when people make reservations online via their website (www.opentable.com). They will also provide you with a simple HTML code (this is the language used to build websites) that you can add to your web site so that people can make reservations directly from your site.

- **Forums:**

An Internet forum is a web application for holding discussions and posting user-generated content.

Forums will allow your clients to post their comments. These comments will be visible to all of the people who access to your website.

Forums could be a great tool to create a sense of community, and will make your clients feel more attached to your place.

To be honest with you, I don't know any restaurants that host forums on their websites (but then again, not many restaurants really deeply care about their clients). They're probably afraid to open a forum on their site and face any negative feedback that they may get.

However, if you are really committed to the Rule of Sincere Caring (review Chapter 1), you should expect good comments and suggestions from the forums on your site.

This is also a great opportunity for you to capture feedback directly from your clients, and to respond humbly and directly to their criticisms. We all make mistakes, and if your potential customers see that you respond sincerely and take measures to improve your business, they will be very willing to forgive and forget your mistakes and reward you with their patronage.

There is nothing worse than a big ego and arrogance to make people avoid your place like the plague.

8. OFFER THEM A MEMBERSHIP CARD:

Some credit card processing companies offer a plastic debit gift cards. These are similar to those offered at Starbucks or department stores.

If you can get these, they can become a great way for you to create client loyalty.

Just ask your credit card processing company to create special cards with your logo and a legend that says: "(Your Restaurant Name) Preferred Client" (of course, replace 'Your Restaurant Name' with the name of your restaurant).

Here is the way that you can use these cards:

Every time that one of your favorite clients returns, at the end of the meal, offer them a free Preferred Client Gift Card and fill it with $20 or $25 (depending on the average price of your menu items and how much money they usually spend at your restaurant).

Tell them that you really appreciate their business and that this card is just a way for you to say *Thank You*.

They will be very happy with the gift and guess where they will go when they go out for dinner? Your place, of course.

They also look better (more elegant) than coupons and gift certificates. Plus, because of their standard card size, people will carry them in their wallets so this opens up the possibilities for them to act spontaneously and stop by your place anytime!

Twenty or twenty-five dollars may seem like throwing money away, but consider that many restaurant owners accept discount programs like the Passport Card as a marketing investment. This card gives the cardholder a free entrée and you don't have control about who uses the card. Many times they are used by people who are looking for a bargain, and who'll spend as little as possible.

Do you start seeing the benefits?

a. You control to whom you give the gift card (only to your best clients).

b. You control the amount to give (a fixed amount of $20 or $25).

c. You invite them to come back, possibly with more people, so $25 is just a small investment to bring back really good clients.

d. They will be very happy and honored to receive this gift from you, and will tell their friends and relatives, increasing the word-of-mouth and your referral promotion system.

If you don't have a plastic gift card, then you can just print special gift cards with the designated value that you can customize with the name of your clients (so that they don't give them to somebody else). Go to Kinko's and get them laminated so that they can use them again. Give them to your best clients at the end of their meals. Not only will they be greatly surprised when they see their names on the card, but they will surely come back to use them!

So there you have it: plenty of ideas designed to bring you repeated clients. Of course, you can use your imagination and come up with many more ideas similar to these (and by the way, if you would like to share them with me, I would be very happy to hear from you, just send me an email to jose@riescoconsulting.com).

If you implement just one of them, you may be able to increase the frequency of visits of your clients by at least 10%; however, if you combine several techniques together, you'll multiply your success rate several percentage points, following the rule of geometric growth that we covered in Chapter 7.

Bringing back your best clients is a great way to fill your tables with valuable and committed patrons who love your place and who'll spread the word about your restaurant, bringing you additional food-loving visitors just like them.

H O M E W O R K

Go back to your reservation books and start creating a list with your best clients.

You can download the Excel template *Clients Database.xls* from my website **www.myrestaurantmarketing.com** (you'll need to subscribe to get access to the download area) and fill in as much information as you can.

During the next 3 months, approach your best clients and fill in the missing information.

1. Create three different Gift Certificates:

   • Inactive Former Clients Gift Certificates

   • Birthday Gift Certificates

   • Preferred Client Gift Card

Call former clients that once frequented your restaurant and offer them the special mail-in Inactive Former Client Gift Certificate

2. Notify your staff about these three new Gift Certificates/Cards. Make sure that they understand their purpose, and encourage them to offer the cards and honor them once presented. Tell them about the special Inactive Former Client Gift Certificates, and explain that they should treat these former clients with Red Carpet treatment.

3. Create a list of strategies that you will implement to bring back your current best clients.

4. Analyze your website (if you have one) or ask to create one if you don't have a site. Work out a design on paper including which components you would like to have. If you have a site, compare these features with what you currently have.

5. Contact your web designer/provider and ask them to make the changes.

6. If you are not happy with your current webmaster, or you want to re-design your Website from scratch, look for a reliable company to do it for you. In the Recommended Resources in my web site: http://myrestau rantmarketing.com/Resources/page24.html,

you'll find some reliable webmasters. Tell them what you want and need on your website.

7. Think about your newsletter. Do you have one? If so, are you using it to the extent that you can?

   If not, are you planning to start one?

   If you don't want to do the job, you can always outsource this task. Again, I've added some additional resources in the resources link (http://myrestaurantmarketing.com/Resources/page24.html) that could help you design, create and maintain your own newsletter.

   You need to decide: How many copies are you going to print? Where are you going to distribute them?

8. Organize a brainstorming session with your employees and ask them about new ideas to increase the frequency of your clients' visits. Not only they will get involved and participate, but you will be surprised how many new ideas they can bring to the table.

Afterword

In the End, It's All About People

You have completed our book. Congratulations!

You now have an incredible advantage over your competitors. You know exactly what to do and why you should do it. You have a clear vision about where do you want to go and how to get there.

I can guarantee you that 99% of all the business owners don't have this advantage, and this roadmap that you have now. They probably never even thought about reflecting for a moment upon their goals and strategies.

Most business owners simply run their business day-to-day, extinguishing fires, jumping from problem to problem without a clear vision. It's like starting a road trip without having a map or a purpose; you can drive around the whole day without knowing where you're going or not reaching any destination.

http://www.myrestaurantmarketing.com

I hope that you found these chapters incredibly informative and full of good ideas that will help you to escalate your business and bring it to the next level.

If you only implement one quarter of all the strategies, techniques and ideas that I gave you in these chapters, you will be well on your way to dramatically improve the performance of your restaurant. If you absorb, adapt and implement a half or more - the sky's the limit!

I also hope that you found this book worthwhile. Like you, I deeply care about my clients and **you** are my client. I trust that you also realized that the first chapters are essential to implementing the changes that you need to multiply your business, and making it more enjoyable for you.

If, after reading the book, you can remember just one thing from all the chapters, please remember this:

You need to put your clients in front of your needs.

There is a Law called the **Law of Compensation**. It reads something like this:

"When you create a benefit for another person, without particular regard for your own well-being, you

create a subconscious desire in the other person to repay you, to create a benefit for you."

In everything that you do, your purpose should be to help make someone's life better.

You are in a unique position - a privileged position - because you own a privileged business: you own a business where people go for pleasure. They are looking forward to having a good time.

Many people give money to professionals to get their taxes done, or to get legal or medical assistance. These are needs that they need to cover, but your place is different.

People visit your restaurant looking for an experience, wanting to have a great time.

People don't go to your restaurant looking for good food (although this is part of the experience) they go looking for a feeling. They want to feel good; they want to feel "special" and if you fail to deliver, they will hit you hard because when you disappoint people, their response is sometimes not a logical response, it is an emotional one. This is why some people react strongly to an unpleasant situation more than somebody else who would consider the disappointment as not very important: they don't act logically, they act emotionally.

Your job is to provide them with a great emotional experience, to make them feel great, to make them feel special.

You are in the driver's seat to giving them happiness.

Don't fail them! And if you do, apologize and compensate them appropriately. You will be lavishly rewarded for your efforts.

Never take people for granted

Don't assume that you can keep relationships with your clients at no cost to you. The greatest secret to growing and sustaining relationships (and bringing you personal and financial success) is to keep reinvesting in the people who surround you.

Many restaurant owners think that once their "visitors" have paid their bills and waved goodbye the relationship is all done.

Nothing can be farther from the truth.

That's why we learned in this book:

- How important is to keep track of your clients.

- How important it is to send them a gift certificate for their birthday.

- How important is to give them gift cards to show them that you really appreciate their business and their company.

- How important is to send them interesting information in your newsletters.

- How important is to remind them whenever you have something special to offer at your place...

If you only care about your profits, if you don't attend to the needs or well-being of your clients, if you don't continuously render a greater and greater value and level of service, if you don't fulfill their needs and provide a great dining experience, somebody else will.

Somebody else will take care of them. And guess what?

They will gladly give their money to that somebody else.

Don't let somebody else grab your clients. You owe to your clients to provide them with the best service, the best food, the best ambience and the best dining experience that they can get anywhere.

If you do this, not only will you be financially rewarded, but you'll also feel good about yourself, about your job, and about your entire life.

You will receive much more than you give. I promise you.

And now, before I say farewell, there is a little surprise for you. I am always looking for feedback. (Yes, I practice what I preach). If you can spend a couple of minutes telling me what you thought about the book, I will give you a wonderful free e-book: **Think and Grow Rich** by Napoleon Hill.

If you follow the principles outlined in **Think and Grow Rich**, you will have mastered the secret of true and lasting success. If you only read only one motivational book this year, please make sure that is **Think and Grow Rich**.

This book is a source of inspiration and a must-read for any businessperson, and it's yours for a few minutes of your feedback.

Please enter the link below in your Internet browser. When the page with the form appears, please enter your email, your name and a few words of feedback about this book (don't worry, I can also take constructive feedback!); you'll be redirected immediately to a page where you'll be able to download a free electronic version of **Think and Grow Rich**.

To get it, go here:
www.myrestaurantmarketing.com/bookgift.html

And don't forget to read my monthly newsletters, weekly blogs and participate in the forum. You can find all of this free of charge at: www.myrestaurantmarketing.com

Good luck and do your best!

Jose L Riesco

INDEX

A

additional merchandise, 253, 272

advantage over your competitors, 52

advertisement placement, 176

ambiance, 59

applications. *See* Software applications

appointments, 281

appropriate compensation, 38,-39

areas of Improvement, 197

art, 73, 267

assets, 150-151, 160

attracting the best workers, 138

attracting new clients, 225

average cost, 250

average sale, 250

B

background music, 268

bad experience, 26-27, 92

bad reputation. *See* reputation: bad

bad reviews, 29, 38, 40

barrier of acquisition, 78

barter opportunity, 166

bartering, 124, 163

One on One, 166-170

Triangulation, 170-184

bartering Possibilities, 184-185

Bento, 232, 279

beers, 72, 199, 257

benefit to your clients,

best clients, 111

birthday certificates, 290

blog, 27, 30, 40, 88, 89, 315-317, 333

blogger, 27

bookkeeping, 122-123

bringing back former clients, 218, 322

building a list, 232

business meetings, 152, 154

C

calendar, 279, 281, 291

carry-out orders, 265

catering business, 153,

    Start/Promote, 254, 268-272

Chamber of Commerce, 142, 184

challenge, 19

change, 13, 15, 20, 86, 106, 112, 117, 119, 133, 202, 224, 254

charitable dinners, 298

clients, 21-25, 31, 35, 37-39, 43, 48, 56, 62, 64-67, 78-88, 91-94, 126-129, 151

    caring, 21

    damage control, 40

    database, 232-233, 236, 275, 288, 291, 294

    definition, 24, 219

    Excel template, 289

    feeling special, 21-22, 32, 52, 53, 57

    frustrated, 23

    happy, 23, 86

    information, 26, 60

    loyalty, 32, 57

    recurrent, 219, 221

    re-engineering your business around, 34

    sympathize, 25, 39, 45

    unhappy, 26, 27, 33, 38, 40, 56, 91, 98, 100,274

client vs. customer (difference), 24

cocktails

    special, 257

collecting

    coupons, 229, 235

communications, 201

compensating

    your clients, 92, 93, 100, 141, 222

    your employees, 156, 189, 255

Compensation (Law of), 328

computer savvy, 232, 235

conference rooms, 152, 154, 155

conferences, 152, 154, 155, 158

conserves, 259

contacts, 154, 161, 188, 202, 229, 261, 275, 281, 284, 286, 311

    Import from Excel, 279

    Information. *See* Website: contact information

cooking classes, 263-264

cost, 91, 146, 165, 175-177, 209, 213, 223, 246, 285, 313

    average, 250

    of gift certificates, 241, 245, 249

    lowering your, 142

coupons, 112, 114, 157, 144-145, 227-230, 300, 312

    adding your USP into, 65

    targeted mailing, 235

    using in advertising campaign, 144

    using in bartering, 167, 178, 180

CRM. *See* Customer Relationship Management Tools

Customers, 24, 91-92

    ask for feedback, 61, 71

    attracting new, 226, 228

    bad for business, 88, 90

    calling former, 286

    converting them into clients, 222-223, 227

    definition, 24, 219

    disgruntled. *See* unhappy

    fears, 80

    frustrated, 23, 27

    response, 144

    unhappy, 26, 31, 33, 40, 91

Customer Relationship Management Tools, 280-282

customer vs. client (difference), 24, 219

customer vs. prospect (difference), 219

D

damage, 56

    credibility, 257

    control, 40

    reputation, 56

undo, 27

database,

capture clients information, 314

create a, 155, 232-233, 275, 282

Excel database, 289, 323

use, 236, 288, 289, 291, 294

deficiencies, 120

degustation menu, 256

delegate, 124, 156, 160

desserts, 256, 258

detail-oriented, 123

differentiate your business, 48, 52, 62, 65, 106, 266

dining experience, 134, 226

dishes,

best sellers, 123, 143, 147, 212

expensive ingredients in, 261

less profitable, 213

most expensive, 209

most profitable, 123, 143

new, 149

originality, 72, 256

selection of, 71

simple, 264

worst sellers, 212

distributors, 198, 199, 202, 257,

big, 260, 261

wine, 293

dream, 104-105, 107-108, 115, 133

E

easy to navigate. *See* Website: requirements

easy to update and maintain. *See* Website: requirements

electronic newsletter. *See* Newsletter: electronic

eliminating risk. *See* risk: eliminating

emotional experience, 23, 25

emotional reasons. *See* emotional experience

employee evaluation form, 44

employee evaluation sheet, 49

employee training program, 139-140, 159

employees, 38, 114, 159

brainstorming with, 325

compensation, 40, 156

efficiency, 192

evaluating, 44, 49-50, 80, 200

excellent, 44, 200

delegating, 155, 160, 188, 285

featured, 301

feedback, 71, 242

happy, 42, 47

leveraging, 123, 138-141, 153, 155

motivated, 203

promises to, 35

respect, 34

sharing, 75

skills, 155

training, 86, 150, 159, 204

unhappy, 43

USP: communicate to, 64, 65, 68, 206

weak, 42-43

Excel. *See* Microsoft Excel

Excel template, 279, 323

excellence, 19, 34, 44, 48, 124, 201, 208, 247, 269

employee evaluation, 49

glimpses of, 121

in service, 270

exotic oils, 262

expensive, 55,

advertising, 225

attracting new clients, 249

cooking books, 263

coupons, 229

dishes, 209

ingredients, 214, 261

printed newsletter, 304

software, 232, 277

F

fears. *See* customers' fears

feedback, 37, 41, 89, 93, 158, 201, 226, 267, 271, 311, 319, 332

FileMaker, 232

finances, 198, 212,

financial statements, 212

follow up, 35, 38, 88, 288

food cost, 165, 180, 183, 209, 213, 246

food to go, 265

Formalized Referral System, 112, 238-240

former client's gift certificates. *See* gift certificates: for former clients

forums, 31, 38-39, 88, 318-319, 333

free food,

free meal,

    abusing the offer, 88, 90

    as part of your USP, 82, 86

    clients asking for, 87

    clients not daring to ask for, 99

    giving, 70, 85, 93, 112, 221, 234

guarantee, 88

offering, 76

    when no to offer, 84

frequency of visits, 112, 193, 217, 224, 226, 271, 273, 280, 284, 322, 325

front of the house, 198, 200

funnel, 223

graphics, 148, 170, 177, 196, 224, 309, 316

G

gathering information about your clients, 60, 232-233, 275-276, 309, 314

    step-by-step system, 283-284

gift certificates, 237-238,

    for former clients, 289-291, 323

    referral, 241-242, 243-245

giving free meals, 112

goal, 109, 112, 132, 191, 211, 227

goods. *See* goods or services.

goods or services,

    buying, 24, 186

getting without money, 163-164,

needing, 166-167, 172, 185, 187

selling, 186

trading, 188

Google, 28, 233, 257, 296, 311, 317

Calendar, 291

Docs, 278

great dining experience, 83

groups, 127, 245, 251, 281

growing your business, 218

growth, 195, 197

exponential, 196

geometric, 191, 244

linear, 196

guarantee, 69, 77, 87, 95, 146

money back, 83, 86, 88, 227

guaranteed excellent dining experience, 82, 94

H

half price, 237

hands off marketing, 229

happy clients. *See* clients: happy

highest

number of clients, 112, 145

performing businesses, 112

quality people, 43

rated restaurants, 83

value, 32

homework, 16, 17, 49, 58, 61, 69, 71, 96, 97, 132, 159, 187, 215, 250, 272, 323

hosting events, 155

hungry people, 56, 57, 203

I

impact

of the marketing, 10

of your service, 72

of your USP, 63

on your business, 192

on your life, 116

on people, 28

on the results, 145

improvements, 15, 16, 19, 118

increasing

number of menu items, 255

price of your menu, 254

the number of clients, 142, 194, 215, 245

the size of your list, 317

the word of mouth about your restaurant, 321

your profit margin, 142

your restaurant's exposure, 315

your revenue, 165

integrity, 34

inventory, 160, 261

Italian restaurant, 45, 60, 186, 211

iWorks, 277, 278

J

Join Ventures (JV), 226, 236

K

kitchen staff, 198, 201

L

labels, 210

art, 267

color coded, 211

food, 210

mailing, 233, 236

wine, 210

with restaurant logo, 259, 262

lack of

distribution, 305

freedom, 118

knowledge, 210, 308

money, 118

quality, 260

strategic thinking, 118

time, 118

Law of Compensation, 328

leadership, 139

leverage, 137

leveraging your:

assets, 150, 158, 163

clients,

distributors,

effort, 138

employees, 138

food, 165, 186

leadership, 139

marketing, 142, 145

name and reputation, 142

operations, 138

other professionals

place, 151

providers,

results, 144

sales, 142

techniques, 158, 163

testing, 143

USP, 142

leveraging possibilities, 150

Lifetime Value of a Client, 220-221, 225, 245

how to calculate, 250-251

live music, 72, 295

local professionals, 231, 235

location, 22, 60, 61, 71, 73, 74, 79, 281

lowering the barrier for consumers, 78, 94

loyalty, 32, 43, 57, 319

M

Mac computers, 232, 277, 279, 302

mail merge, 233

mailing,

coupons, 230

direct, 184

gift certificates, 288, 290

labels, 236

list, 305

postcards, 298

printed newsletter, 304

targeted, 230, 234

Marginal Net Worth (MNW)

of a client, 223

of a restaurant, 222

market segmentation, 127, 129

marketing,

basic rule of, 77

budget, 146, 218, 219, 220

campaign, 126, 127, 138, 143, 150, 219

contacts, 281

coupons, 226, 229

efforts, 144

expenses, 146, 229, 273, 313

genius, 143

groups, 129

hands off,

initiatives, 228

internet, 211

investment, 226, 229, 234, 238, 247, 321

leverage, 142, 146

local, 128

materials, 171, 205, 241

measurable, 225

message, 205

online, 308

people, 200

platform, 272

profits, 220

programs, 142

risk-free, 249

sales (and), 159, 198

segmentation, 129

spending, 28

strategies, 143, 205, 226, 239, 285

testing, 143, 146

tools, 130, 143, 239, 241

training, 276

USP, 53, 54, 65, 66, 75

variables, 146

vehicles, 130, 225, 238, 240, 306

material assets *See* assets

measurable, 225, 229, 235

meeting place, 154

meeting planners, 154, 155

membership cards, 319

menu,

    choices, 249

    cocktail, 257

    degustation, 256

    dishes, 143, 149, 210, 212, 213, 256

ethnic, 71

items, 59, 86, 143, 192, 214, 253-254, 272, 294, 299, 320

prices, 85, 149, 191, 244, 253-254

selection, 71

special, 256

testing, 149, 150

Microsoft Access, 232

Microsoft CRM, 282

Microsoft Excel, 276, 277

Microsoft Office, 263, 276, 277, 278, 291

Microsoft Publisher, 263, 302

Microsoft Windows, 232

Microsoft Word, 263

mineral water, 255, 256

miscommunication, 139, 159

N

negative

comments, 39

experiences, 27, 89

feedback, 40, 89, 319

publicity, 26, 31

reviews, 28, 87,

word of mouth, 31

networking, 226

clients, 157, 161, 314

opportunities, 130, 157

professional groups, 142, 231, 298

Social, 26

newsletters, 53, 65, 171, 184, 202, 295, 300-306, 314

blogs (as an alternative to), 316

content, 302, 331

electronic, 276, 284, 304-305

design, 302

information, 302

printed, 303-304

registration, 312

resources, 325

scheduling, 281

template, 302

Web site, 315

notes, 13, 16, 17, 280, 281, 284

O

obstacles, 79, 81

offers, 145

in coupons, 227

no combined with other, 242

to your potential clients, 312

Office. *See* Microsoft Office

online

applications. *See* online: software applications

blogs, 88, 316

calendar, 291

commenting, 27

content (finding), 301

database, 279

food products, 260

forums, 88

list, 233

marketing, 308

postcards, 230

posting, 27

presence, 278

professionals, 231, 296

promoting your restaurant, 308

recipes, 257

registrations, 154

reservations, 310 317-318

restaurant guides, 38

reviews, 41, 83, 208

selling, 262

software applications, 278, 291

wine list, 310

Yellow Pages, 231

Open Office, 277

operations, 11, 57, 104-105, 115, 116-119, 138, 140, 198, 204-205

day to day, 58, 95, 103, 109, 117

difference from strategy, 113

employees (and), 159

leverage your, 138

re-evaluate your, 197

transforming your, 109

underperforming, 197

opportunities, 111, 259

networking, 130

new, 158, 161

sales, 262

undiscovered, 197

optimal performance, 121

optimization, 111

over-delivering, 35

P

personal life, 115, 117

plastic gift card, 319, 321

poetry reading, 296-297

point-of-sale system, 212

policies

implementing, 287

large distributor, 200

setup, 86

written, 141

possibilities for

a bad experience, 85

bartering, 184, 186

creating a USP, 54, 56

creative, 169

leveraging, 150-152, 157-158

working together with other people, 160

postcards, 53, 65, 227, 230, 233, 235-236, 276

preserves, 186, 259-260, 264

price

average, 207, 320

discounted, 167, 181

full, 167

gift certificates (of), 214

half, 237

high, 255

in USP, 54

increasing, 148, 179, 191, 213, 253-255

lowering, 148

of your dishes, 148-149, 165

of your menu, 55, 150, 254, 256, 310

perfect, 254

premium, 183

retail, 177, 228

sales, 175

testing your, 84, 146-148

wine, 211

printed newsletter. *See* newsletter: printed

priorities, 121, 125, 249

process, 107, 127, 241

daily, 150

elimination, 212

food ordering, 212

gathering client information, 286, 314

improvements, 84, 86, 118, 138, 197, 201

main, 198

optimize, 139, 202

postcard creation, 233

review, 199

unclear, 139, 141, 159, 200

written, 204

professional goals, 115

professionals,

associations, 152

dealing with, 151, 157, 160, 161

directories, 231

events for, 297

outsourcing to, 122

partnership with, 142

targeting your mailing to, 231, 235

profession-specific events,

profit margin,

from each dish, 123, 209

increasing, 112, 258

maintaining, 213

testing, 147

tracking, 123, 146, 187, 246

promises,

fulfilling, 56, 61, 67

in your USP, 67

promotions,

advertise your, 300, 306

credibility of , 27

email, 312

materials, 65

offering, 299

referral system, 321

testing, 145-146

to fill in weak days, 300

USP, 65

prospects, 38, 62,

bringing, 218, 227, 236, 238

definition, 219

difference with clients and customers, 219

fears, 79, 80

high income, 230

list building, 232

providers, 20, 35, 42, 53, 58, 61, 65, 109, 133, 151

bartering with, 186

leveraging, 156, 160, 161

purchase amount, 253, 271

Q

Quick

cooperation with other business owners, 237

dealing with a problem, 92

following with your clients, 38

learning, 120

lunch, 55

promoting, 143

R

R.S.V.P, 227, 179

radio stations, 173-174, 178-179, 183, 299

ranking

your employees, 44, 49-50

your strengths, 119-125

recipes, 262, 301, 315

books, 262, 301

in your website, 315

recommended software. *See* Software

referral, 161

    benefits from using, 239-240

    formalized system, 112 , 238-249

    gift certificates, 112

    promotion system, 321

    software, 313

referral-generated client, 240

refunds, 40, 70

registration form, 312

repetition, 18

reputation,

    bad, 31

    damage to, 56

    good, 34-36, 231

    leverage your, 142

respect, 33, 34, 43, 203

Restaurant Marginal Net Worth. *See* Marginal Net Worth: of a restaurant

restaurant policy workbook, 101

reviews,

competitors, 134

online, 28 ,38, 40, 41, 83, 87, 208

risk,

    eliminating, 78, 81, 83, 92-95, 249, 294

    minimizing, 111

    reducing, 143

    zero *See* Zero Risk Transactions

MNW. *See* Marginal Net Worth: of a restaurant

roles and responsibilities, 138, 140, 141, 159

Rule of Sincere Caring, 21, 61, 319

rules,

    basic for USP, 67

    following 11, 12, 115

    new, 106

    of marketing, 77

    powerful, 215

    segmentation, 129

S

sales,

additional, 147, 165, 255, 268, 269

and excellence, 17

and income, 19

and marketing, 11, 75, 198, 205

and profits, 148, 226, 271

comparison, 148

dishonest techniques, 32

force, 94, 95, 139, 200

increasing, 14, 41, 77, 146, 186

letters, 145, 230

levels, 254

merchandise, 266

opportunities, 262

pressure, 226, 267, 271

price, 175

results, 144, 147, 148

wine, 157

salesmen, 218

satisfaction,

clients, 226, 270

guarantee, 98, 146

sauces, 264

scenarios, 83, 87-88, 98-99

second

list, 73

option, 106

time, 39

try, 38

seminars, 152, 158, 160

service

bad, 23, 29, 41, 46, 87, 92

excellent, 10, 23, 37, 41, 72, 84, 126, 247, 255, 270

importance of your, 29, 39, 208, 220, 287, 292, 293

in your USP, 54

quality of, 85, 93, 200, 243

mediocre, 21

provider, 167, 170, 181, 188

services. *See* goods or services.

Simpleology, 116,

skills,

employees (of your), 44, 123, 151, 157, 160, 188

leveraging

    from professionals, 157

    your staff's, 155, 157

    your providers, 156

    special, 121

small portion desserts, 257

Social Networking, 26,

software,

    CRM, 280

    free, 277

    Mac. *See* Mac

    Microsoft. *See* Microsoft

    open source, 277

    recommended, 276, 277

    tell-a-friend, 313

    to track your clients, 276

special

    and different, 53, 71

    beers, 72, 257

    benefits, 73

cards, 320, 321

clients, 189

cocktails, 257, 301

consideration, 57

events, 225

dessert, 256

dinning, 25

discounts, 233

events, 293, 297, 310

feeling, 21

gift certificates, 289, 323, 324

logo, 289

menus, 55, 66, 256, 293

moment, 32

motivation, 52

occasion, 32, 66, 73, 112, 256

offering, 52, 65, 294, 331

person, 32

promotions, 146

referral gift certificates, 241, 243, 244, 248

sauce, 264

skills, 121, 307

something, 11, 52

strategies. See strategies: special

treat, 259

treatment, 289, 290

your restaurant (is), 52, 53, 61, 62, 71

wines, 72, 157, 210, 257, 294

spice mixes, 264

staff. See employees

statistics, 26, 123, 307

strategic

advantage, 137

decision, 126, 129

mindset, 15, 95

partnerships, 142

thinking, 118,

strategy, 15,

and operations, 113

and positioning, 57

and vision, 107, 109-115, 115, 140

business, 110

creating, 110, 112, 113

current, 112

developing, 105

reactive, 110

ultimate, 112, 150

strengths, 95, 120-121, 124

suggestions

and ideas, 159, 202

and recommendations, 19

box, 311

of events, 293

T

target

audience, 129, 130, 144, 229, 230, 232, 234-235

define, 126

events, 130

list, 233

mailing, 234

market, 126

marketing, 128, 223, 231

reaching, 104

your USP, 62, 65

targeting

a special occasion, 66

a group, 129-130, 297

meeting planners, 154

your clientele, 128-130, 229

targeted mailing, See mailing: targeted

tasks, 121-124

accomplishing, 121-122, 156, 213

and activities, 121

challenging, 156

compensate for, 156

delegate, 123, 124, 160, 188, 232, 236, 285

focusing on, 122

improvement, 198, 213

outsourcing, 276, 325

software (using), 277, 281

struggling with, 123, 157

television, 179

Think and Grow Rich, 332-333

third party, 169,173, 284

food products, 260

tight budget, 163

tips,

and ideas, 13, 14, 218

and recommendations, 15

from clients, 43

lost, 92, 101, 156

management, 141

top priorities, 121

total satisfaction, 70

triangulation bartering. See bartering: triangulation

TV advertising, 128, 130, 172, 225

U

unhappy clients. See clients: unhappy

Unique Selling Proposition, 11, 51-80

articulating, 63

creating, 54, 59, 62

basic rules, 67-68

building into your marketing, 53, 54, 65, 70, 205

catering (creating a USP for), 270

communicating, 140, 64-65, 75

creating, 54, 56, 71, 74-75

definition, 52

fulfilling, 86

integrating in your communications, 70, 101

living your, 68, 80, 86

suggestions, 55, 71-72

selecting, 67

step by step creation, 59

using with promotions, 65

writing, 74, 101, 140, 141

USP. *See* Unique Selling Proposition

V

value of a client. *See* Lifetime Value of a Client

value

and quality of your offerings, 32, 59

core values, 34

cost, 180

for your clients, 108, 237, 251, 288

of gift certificates, 164, 245, 322

of your food, 238

reputation, 36

retail, 167, 178

services, 175, 331

wines, 209

vendors, 40, 122, 150, 260

VIP treatment, 290

vision,

and a plan, 95

changing, 15

creating, 95, 106, 132-133

definition, 104-105

developing a strategy to reach your, 105, 109

having, 103-110, 129

living, 206, 327

marketing, 205

process to reach your, 107, 132-133

questions to define your, 108

refining, 106

sharing, 139, 159

statement, 105

steps to take, 133

understanding your, 113

writing, 140

Vista Print, 233

W

weaknesses, 64, 120, 122, 135

web design company,

website,

advertise in, 300

analyze, 324

attractive, 308

blog, 315-317

calendar, 281

catering menu, 269

capturing clients information, 233

contact information, 311

create, 307

CRM, 282

design, 156

easy to navigate, 309

easy to update, 311

forums, 38, 318

full of content, 310

marketing, 202

newsletters (posting), 305, 314

online reservations, 317

photos, 315

posting your USP, 53, 65

registration form, 312

requirements, 308-319

recipes, 315

reviews, 28, 40, 208

templates (download from my site), 323

to create cookbooks, 262

simple, 309

Simpleology, 116

suggestions box, 311

update, 306

videos, 315

Windows.   *See*   Microsoft Windows

wine

additional sales, 165

book, 210

color coded, 210-211

complementary, 256

cost, 209

description, 210

dessert, 210

dinners, 293, 310

distributor, 157, 199, 293

excellent, 209

exciting, 293

label, 210

lack of knowledge, 210

limited availability, 257

list, 210-211, 310

markup, 55

names (pronunciation), 211

new, 294

offer food with, 258

ordering, 211

pairing (with food), 210-211

region, 301

sales, 210-211, 259

selection, 54, 71, 72, 74

special, 146, 294

tasting event, 66, 157

value, 209

wireless,

access, 153

connection, 152

router, 153

setup connection, 155

Y

yearning, 120

Yellow Pages, 10, 112, 130, 167, 206-208, 225, 231, 235, 298

Z

Zero Risk Transactions, 77

LaVergne, TN USA
31 March 2011
222357LV00001B/70/P